THE SHADIER GARDEN

THE SHADIER GARDEN

HARRIET L. CRAMER

CRESCENT
BOOKS
New York • Avenel

A FRIEDMAN GROUP BOOK

This 1997 edition is published by Crescent Books,
a division of Random House Value Publishing, Inc.
40 Engelhard Avenue, Avenel, New Jersey 07001.

Crescent Books and colophon are trademarks of Random House Value Publishing, Inc.

Random House
New York • Toronto • London • Sydney •Auckland

Editor: Susan Lauzau
Art Director: Lynne Yeamans
Designer: Jan Melchior
Photography Editor: Kathryn Culley

Color separations by COLORSCAN OVERSEAS CO PTE LTD
Printed in China by Leefung-Asco Printers Ltd.

Library of Congress Cataloging-in-Publication Data.

Cramer, Harriet L.
    The shadier garden : inspiration and techniques, comprehensive
plant encyclopedia, complete design plans / Harriet L. Cramer
    p. cm.
    ISBN 0-517-14273-2
    1. Gardening in the shade. 2. Shade-tolerant plants. 1. Title.
SB434.7.W48   1997   96-36596
635.9'54--dc20

9 8 7 6 5 4 3 2 1

CONTENTS

I have often wondered if the way I came to appreciate gardening in the shade is atypical. For years I tried to convince myself that I did indeed have a sunny garden. Perhaps this is because my ideal garden revolved around sun-loving perennial borders and wildflower meadows. For a very long time a garden was for me, almost by definition, a planting of flowers or vegetables in a sunny location. Now, the fact that my perennial border was flanked on one side by a mature red maple and on another side by my neighbor's two flowering dogwood trees gives an indication of my advanced state of denial about the amount of sunlight the garden actually received. I did notice (I'm not completely dense) that a great many of the plants either refused to flower year after year or arched so visibly toward the sun that they appeared to suffer from the plant version of strained muscles.

As I matured as a gardener and came to appreciate the more subtle elements of design, I finally realized that shade can be a blessing rather than a curse. Because there is a limited palette of boisterously flowering plants to choose from when gardening in the shade, one must rely more on plants that are quietly impressive or even downright nondescript until used in just the right combination. In a shady garden, much more so than in a sunny site, the careful positioning of contrasting and complementary foliage colors, textures, and forms reveals the artistry required to create a successful garden.

Where summers are particularly hot you can grow with some afternoon shade a great many plants that would surely wilt or turn brown in full sun. White-flowering plants and those with variegated foliage can seem harsh or washed out in direct sunlight; in shade they seem almost to glow.

It is in a shaded setting that the quietly dramatic potential of light and shadow can be most fully realized. Consider a walk in the woods, the dappled light accenting patches of ferns or mosses and other woodland plants. It is the contrast, the natural interplay of light and dark, that makes this scene so dazzling.

In a shady site we are in fact presented with perhaps our greatest opportunity to emulate in the garden what is most inspiring to us in nature. Streaks of sunlight breaking through the darkness, the smell and feel of pine needles and decaying leaves underfoot, the diversity of foliage textures and shapes, and the sense of depth and lushness created through the layering of plants—these sensory delights of the woods can all be re-created in the careful design of a shady garden.

Another obvious advantage of a shady site became apparent to me this past summer. For weeks the daytime temperatures hovered in the upper 90s and the sun was unrelenting. Working day after day in a shadeless, formal rose garden, the allure of roses fading even faster than the suffering blossoms, I felt very close to becoming seriously deranged. This is a public garden, so I tried not to

WHAT IS SHADE?

lash out with sharp tools or chemical sprays at the visitors who would ask, "Is it hot enough for you?" As I toiled away in this hellish environment I thought often about how the joy of gardening lies not just in the final product, for surely no serious gardener ever considers a garden to be finished, but in the process of gardening. This process is distinctly more enjoyable when you are working in an environment not conducive to heatstroke. Where summers are hot, a shady garden allows us to enjoy not just the garden but the very act of gardening.

A shaded spot in the garden will also be a welcome refuge to butterflies, birds, and other animals. Many of these creatures need some quiet shade in which to shelter and nest, and even a small bit of shade may entice them to the garden. This is especially pleasing at a time when our gardens seem year after year to be ever more devoid of beneficial wildlife.

Above: **The trees and shrubs in your shady garden will act as a beacon for birds, like this American goldfinch.** *Opposite*: **This mass of white-flowered snowdrops, blooming under a canopy of deciduous trees, is a truly uplifting sight in late winter.**

This is a more complicated question than it may first appear to be. Shade is not the absence of sunlight, but a lesser quantity and perhaps quality of sunlight. The opposite of shade isn't "sun" as much as it is "full sun." If full sun is commonly considered to be five to six hours of direct sunlight per day, then a garden with anything less than this can be considered in a broad sense to be shady. What becomes critical to determine is how much sunlight your garden receives, between what hours of the day your garden is shadiest and sunniest, whether the light is direct or indirect, how much the quantity and intensity of light changes through the seasons in your climate, the orientation of your garden, and the sources of your shade.

Begin analyzing your situation by looking at what causes your garden to be shady. Is your plot shaded by a building, wall, or other architectural structure? Is the shade created by tall trees? Are they deciduous or evergreen? The shade cast by an evergreen—continuous, though with subtle seasonal variations because of the changing angle of the sun in the sky—is very different from that of a deciduous tree. The nature and degree of shade created by a deciduous tree will vary tremendously depending upon, among other factors, how dense, high, and widespreading the canopy of that particular tree is. Before you plant in the shade you should also try to imagine what the ultimate size of your shade trees will be, how fast they are likely to grow, and how the garden will be affected by their growth.

Once you have identified the sources of shade in your garden you need to understand the nature of the shade you have and how it changes over time. Different books use different classifications of shade and these can become quite complex. Intricate charts tracking azimuth angles and foot-candles of light may be intellectually interesting but are not necessarily helpful to the gardener who simply wants to understand what will grow well in his or her particular garden. I prefer the relatively straightforward division of shade into four categories, namely partial, light, full, and dense shade.

These classifications are meant to facilitate rather than dictate your planting decisions. There may well be an ideal magnitude, duration, and direction of light for each plant, but this does not mean that the plant will perform well only under optimum conditions. Most plants will, if other circumstances are favorable, tolerate multiple gradations of light.

A garden with partial shade actually receives quite a lot of sunshine. It may have direct sun in the morning or in the afternoon, or the sun might come and go throughout the course of the day. There is no precise definition of partial shade in terms of number of hours of sunlight, but the assumption is that the garden will receive at least a few hours of direct sunlight each day.

Morning sun and afternoon shade is an almost perfect situation. There are many plants that need some direct sunshine to grow and flower but tend to suffer in the hot light of a summer afternoon. Many of the herbaceous and woody plants that we commonly think of as sun-loving are in

Combinations of plants like these grasses, hostas, and ferns offer a lush, textured look to the shade garden, maintaining visual interest even when no flowers are in bloom.

fact much happier in partial shade, especially if you live in a warm climate. Columbines, daylilies, Japanese anemones, foxgloves, and coralbells, to name just a few, will bloom over a longer period of time, have brighter-colored flowers, and maintain more attractive foliage if grown in afternoon shade. The same is true for a large number of woody plants, including stewartia, clethra, fothergilla, and chokeberry.

Light shade is distinguished from partial shade by the quality of light. A garden in light shade receives dappled sunlight. The source of shade in this situation is likely to be a deciduous tree with high branches or with small leaves, such as a honey locust or river birch, which allow sunlight to filter down to the lower canopy. "Light shade" would also define a site on the north side of a low building or wall where the strength of the sun is felt mainly through reflection. A garden in the shadow of trees or buildings some distance away is another example of light shade.

The kind of plants you can grow in this situation is greatly determined by the nature of the roots of the trees casting the shade. If the surrounding trees have relatively deep roots, there is a large diversity of woody and herbaceous plants you'll be able to use. Viburnum, dogwood, holly, rhododendron, Solomon's seal, lobelia, alchemilla, and many forms of iris thrive in light shade. A once-blooming climbing rose can even be grown in dappled light if the tree under which it is planted leafs out after the rose has bloomed in the spring.

If the roots of the shade tree are shallow and fibrous, however, like the roots of beeches, maples, and sycamores, it will be difficult to underplant; the soil is

probably too nutrient- and moisture-deprived to allow understory plants to grow well. It is not impossible to plant under such trees, but your choice of plants will be limited to thuglike plants like periwinkle, pachysandra, English ivy, and lilies of the valley.

under Sycamore

When we think of a shady garden, what we usually envision is a site in full shade. Gardens with full shade are shaded throughout the growing season and the shade is roughly constant throughout the day. If your garden is on the north side of the house and there are mature trees nearby, you have a classic full shade situation. Full shade may also exist under tall deciduous trees with low branches and/or an abundant leaf mass as well as under large evergreens.

In full shade, the conditions—other than the limited light—are assumed to be

Above: **The tall flower spikes of foxglove *(Digitalis purpurea)* lift the eye and the spirits in late spring and early summer. This fuzzy-leafed biennial is a good example of a plant that will thrive in either partial shade or full sun. It is perfect in a traditional English cottage garden, in a mixed border, or in an herb garden.**

conducive to plant growth. That is to say, the soil is neither too dry nor too wet, there is adequate air circulation, and the tree roots do not discourage underplanting. A typical eastern woodland—with a diversity of trees of different shapes and sizes and good, loamy soil—is what is meant by full shade. Ferns flourish well here, as will most of the plants we traditionally think of as shade-loving: hostas,

astilbes, cimicifuga, ginger, foamflower, sweet woodruff, and numerous broad-leaved evergreens.

The difference between full and dense shade lies not in the amount of sunlight received (in both cases the site remains largely shaded throughout the day and the growing season), but in the other conditions necessary for plant growth. In full shade these are assumed to be favorable, whereas in dense shade they are not. A good example of dense shade is the shade under a mature white pine, hemlock, or beech tree, where the low branching habit and an impenetrable mass of roots close to the surface discourage underplanting. Another case of dense shade is the relentless shadow cast by a tall building, fence, or hedge. In such an unpromising environment only the toughest ground covers are likely to survive.

11

Above: **The ambiance of a refined woodland is created by underplanting mature deciduous trees with spring-blooming foamflowers (*Tiarella cordifolia*).** *Below left*: **Heucheras, hostas, ferns, and lady's mantle combine to form a rich textural tapestry in the summer garden.** *Below right*: **Hostas are an elegant addition to the shady garden and are available in a mind-boggling diversity of sizes, shapes, and colors.**

THE VARIABILITY OF SHADE

Understanding the causes and nature of the shade in your garden are critical first steps in designing for a shady site. The categories discussed previously will help you identify your specific situation, though classification is by no means the end of the process. Shade is not a static concept. It changes over time and from place to place. The sunlight your garden receives varies with the orientation of your garden, the time of day, the time of year, and your geographic location. How shady your garden is today, moreover, is likely to be different from how shady it will be five years from now as some plants grow and others die. The level of shade in which you garden can also be intentionally altered as trees are thinned, limbed up, or removed entirely.

The location of your garden relative to the movement of the sun in the sky has great significance for the kind of light you receive and the diversity of plants you can grow. If you garden in North America, the sunniest and warmest spot will be (if not blocked by trees or tall buildings) the one with southern exposure. This is true regardless of the time of year, though in midsummer the light will be strongest. Shade-loving plants will generally tolerate a south-facing location only if shaded by trees or shrubs or some architectural structure.

The northern side of the garden, in contrast, is typically well-suited for plants that prefer full or dense shade. This is especially true if the northern

exposure is shaded by large trees or dark-colored walls or buildings.

An eastern exposure is often considered ideal because there, throughout the growing season, the optimum combination of cool morning sun and refreshing afternoon shade will satisfy the vast majority of plants. A west-facing garden with morning shade and afternoon sun offers great possibilities as well, though these may be somewhat reduced in those parts of the country where the heat and light of a summer afternoon are prohibitively harsh.

Obviously, the openness of your specific site influences how important orientation is in the amount of sunlight your garden receives. A south-facing garden shaded by mature oaks is clearly quite different from a garden with the same exposure but without the trees or with other kinds or varying maturities of trees. The impact of orientation will also be affected by the change of seasons if your south-, east-, or west-facing garden is shaded by deciduous trees. A garden that receives shade in the late spring and summer but strong sunlight in winter and early spring might be an ideal place to grow early-flowering plants like hellebores, wild blue phlox, epimediums, lungworts, and bergenias.

A good understanding of the way the light varies depending upon the orientation of the garden and the relative position of the sun increases your likelihood of placing the right plants in the right locations. This is clearly an aspect of gar-

Above: **The prominent leaves of heartleaf bergenia (*Bergenia cordifolia*) turn a warm, glowing mahogany-bronze in the pale light of winter.**
Below: **Stinking hellebore's (*Helleborus foetidus*) chartreuse, bell-shaped flowers emerge in winter when the rest of the garden is quiescent. The flowers persist long into spring— even when not in flower this is an attractive and underutilized plant for deciduous shade.**

13

Japanese camellias, like this 'Adolphe Audusson' cultivar, thrive in light shade in warmer climates. Hundreds of cultivars are available, with an array of flower colors and forms from which to choose.

climate, as well as light quality, that make it so difficult to effectively re-create English-style cottage gardens in many parts of North America. While we habitually consider climate in choosing the plants most likely to be cold hardy for us, we tend to underestimate its role in determining where in the garden these plants are best placed for maximum health and vigor.

Every region has its unique climatic features. Fluctuations in temperature from one season to another and within a season, the level of rainfall, the direction and intensity of winds, the frequency of hurricanes, tornadoes, ice storms, or other metereological extremes—all of these factors influence what and where we can plant. The observant gardener will learn over time which plants must be protected from drying winds or scorching sunlight or whatever weather peculiarities exist in his or her particular area. A shade-loving plant in one region may well be a shade-tolerant plant in another. The wood asters that a gardener in Georgia traditionally grows in full shade, for instance, will accept only very light shade in a garden in Vermont and in fact prefer a great deal of sunshine. An inexperienced gardener or one new to an area would be well advised to talk with local gardeners and nurserymen to understand what kind of weather he or she is likely to encounter and how best to cope.

dening over which we can have real control. The climate in which we garden, on the other hand, is equally important to our ultimate success but not nearly so easy to manage.

The influence of climate upon the garden cannot be overstated. This is evident to anyone who has gardened over time in different latitudes. Climate explains why the delphiniums and

lupines grown in the mid-Atlantic region rarely flower as prolifically or bloom as long as those grown in New England and the Pacific Northwest. Climatic variations, among other factors, explain why conifers generally perform much better in northern than in southern gardens and why the opposite is true of magnolias and many other spring-blooming plants. It is the differences in

BEYOND SUNLIGHT

The nature and intensity of the light in your garden directs you toward the kinds of plants that will theoretically grow well there. Whether or not your garden actually thrives, however, will probably be determined by factors other than sunlight. I have lost more shade-loving plants because of poor drainage than because of too much or too little light. We tend to focus on sunlight because its absence is so obvious in a shady setting, but plants also demand healthy, unobstructed, and well-drained soil; adequate moisture in the air and in the ground; and good air circulation in order to prosper.

As you design your garden in the shade, try to imagine a vigorous woodland. Where plant life is lush and diverse, you notice that the soil feels rich and is neither too dry nor too wet. The air seems comfortably moist and the plants are not packed so tightly together that air is unable to flow around them. The upper canopy of trees may be dense but some sunlight and rainfall is able to filter through to the plants below. The ground is covered by the decaying leaves and needles of the surrounding trees and shrubs. This natural mulch keeps soil temperatures from fluctuating too wildly, provides cool shade for tree roots, and replenishes important nutrients as it decomposes. Regardless of the size of your shady site or your individual landscape objectives, these are the cultural conditions you should try to re-create for your garden to flourish.

SOIL

Anecdotal evidence leads me to believe that poor soil is responsible for more failures in gardening in the shade than any other one factor. Plants derive much of the moisture and nutrients they need from the soil. The soil is also the berth in which their roots are anchored. Ideal soil for a shady garden would be loamy and reasonably well-drained. Its texture would be neither too sandy nor too claylike and its chemistry would be roughly balanced, though a slightly acidic soil is certainly acceptable for most shade-loving plants. The upper level of the soil should be sufficiently friable to dig down several inches and should not be clogged by an arid, impenetrable mass of tree roots.

How do you know if you have the right kind of soil for a shade garden? The easiest way to find out is to dig holes a foot or so deep in several areas of the prospective site and carefully examine the soil. If you are not able to penetrate more than two or three inches (5 to 8cm) because of surface roots, you need to add a few inches of improved soil to what is already there. This additional soil will not harm the tree as long as it is not too deep or heavy or dumped right up against the trunk. Shade-loving herbaceous plants in general do not have very deep roots but they do require a minimum of four to six inches (10 to 15cm) of good soil in order to root and grow.

Assuming you are able to dig down six or more inches (15 or more centimeters), notice the color of the soil you are removing. Is it light or dark? Light-colored soil indicates a lack of humus, the decaying organic material so essential for strong root growth. Humus is dark and rich in nutrients; plants growing under trees gen-

A dreary winter landscape is enlivened by the glorious yellow flowers of Chinese witch hazel (Hamamelis mollis). This is one of the most brilliant of the witch hazels and probably the most fragrant. Like so many shade-loving plants, it will flourish if planted in moist, acidic, well-drained soil that is rich in organic material.

15

erally need added nutrients precisely because their location places them in constant nutritional competition with the trees above. A lack of earthworms would also indicate that there is not enough humus. The soil can be improved by adding a combination of leaf mold (that is, decayed leaves), compost, peat moss, and aged manure. It would be best to so amend the overall site, especially if the soil is truly awful. If you are prevented from doing this because of existing plantings, a mixture of these organic materials should at least be incorporated into the soil when new planting holes are dug.

The texture of your garden soil should also be obvious through examination. On one extreme is sandy soil, which is gritty and porous. This is fine for an herb garden since most herbs prefer a lean, sharply drained soil. Most shade-loving plants will not thrive in sand, however, because such soil loses nutrients and moisture too quickly. The plants may initially grow well if frequently watered but are likely to languish over time unless the soil texture and quality are amended by adding compost, leaf mold, peat moss, additional topsoil, and periodic applications of fertilizer.

A garden with heavy clay soil, the other extreme, can be a nightmare to work with. This kind of soil is very finely textured and will feel smooth and slick. It tends to clump into dense, impervious masses through which water will filter extremely slowly if at all. A garden with such soil seems perpetually too wet or too dry and the subsoil may feel like cement. You can be certain you have clay soil if you dig a good-size hole, fill it with water, and an hour later the water

still has not drained. You can readily imagine that this is not an environment most plants would relish. Over time, the roots of all but the toughest survivors are likely to rot. The solution is again to add as much organic material as possible to the soil before planting; I will often mix gravel in as well to ensure improved drainage.

The chemical balance of your soil, which is measured in terms of acidity or alkalinity, is also a consideration when planting in the shade. If evergreens are native to your area, your soil is probably more acidic than alkaline. If you live in an area with limited rainfall, like much of the western United States, or with significant limestone rock formations, you will tend to have more alkaline soil. A soil test will indicate where your soil falls on the pH scale of 1 to 14; below 7 is acidic, above 7 is alkaline, and a read-

ing of 7 is considered approximately neutral. You may find subtle variations within your property; your soil may, for instance, be generally neutral or acidic but fairly alkaline alongside the foundation of your house or beside a wall where cement has leached lime into the soil over time.

The vast majority of plants are content in a neutral soil, roughly balanced between acidic and alkaline. Some shade-loving plants will definitely prefer an acidic soil, notably members of the ericaceous family like rhododendrons, azaleas, mountain laurels, and heaths and heathers. Few plants for a shady garden actually demand an alkaline soil.

You can alter the chemical balance of your soil to encourage certain kinds of plants that might otherwise be less than content in your garden. Before you attempt any changes, conduct a soil test

WATER

using samples from different areas of your garden. The test kits available at garden centers will give a rough idea of your soil chemistry; for a more detailed analysis and specific recommendations, contact your local Agricultural Extension Service. Soil acidity can be raised by adding sulfur, aluminum sulfate, iron sulfate, or ammonium sulfate in quantities that will vary depending upon your specific situation. A slower but more natural way to acidify your site is to mulch with pine, hemlock needles, or composted oak leaves. If you find your soil to be too acidic you can either apply ground limestone every few years into the soil directly or simply spread it on top.

Organic mulches such as decayed leaves or pine needles are a good way to fertilize your shady garden as well. Plants growing in the shade of nutritionally demanding trees or in the infertile soil alongside a wall need supplemental feeding. As an organic mulch decomposes, it adds valuable nutrients to the soil. Since this is a gradual process, it is advisable to also use a balanced, granular fertilizer once or twice each year. A slow-release fertilizer is fine and is best applied in early spring and again in early summer. Avoid fertilizing much later than midsummer because the new growth the fertilizing encourages may be too tender to survive a difficult winter.

Opposite: **Many woodland wildflowers, such as Japanese primrose (Primula japonica) and wild blue phlox (Phlox divaricata), perform best in the moist soil found along the edge of a pond or stream.** *Right*: **Azaleas prefer an acidic soil with a pH reading of 6.5 or lower.**

Whether plants are grown in sun or shade, they need hydrogen and oxygen from water to survive. We assume that plants growing in full sun need more water than those grown in shade, but this is not necessarily true. Shade-tolerant plants sited beneath mature trees are competing with those trees for the moisture in the soil and in the air. Trees with dense canopies will absorb a particularly large share of the available rainfall through their foliage, leaving less for the understory plants. The roots of the trees—especially moisture-loving trees like maples, sycamores, and tulip trees— also soak up vast quantities of water.

Depending upon your climate, an inch (2½ cm) of rain a week through the growing season will usually be enough for most shade gardens as long as this

rain is truly filtering down to the herbaceous and small woody plants. A rain gauge is useful to monitor rainfall, but an even better method is to regularly feel the soil just below the surface to ensure that it is always moist (not soggy). Because the shade-creating canopy can act like an umbrella and because of the voracious thirst of the tree roots, you will probably need to water your shade garden periodically. When you do water, use a soaker hose rather than a sprinkler because the former will ensure that the needed moisture reaches the roots of the plants.

A top dressing (a light covering, approximately 1 inch [2½ cm] thick) of mulch or leaf mold will help conserve moisture, as well as regulate soil temperature and discourage weeds. Which kind of mulch or leaf mold you use is largely a

AIR

In addition to healthy soil and sufficient moisture, plants must have enough air circulating around them to allow their foliage to dry and to permit sunlight to filter through. If plants are crowded together they will grow sparse and leggy and will be far more prone to disease. Air circulation becomes a problem either when too many plants are crowded too close together or when the branches of the sheltering trees are growing so dense and low to the ground that air cannot flow sufficiently around and through the understory plants.

To improve the air circulation in your garden, you can judiciously prune some trees and shrubs and remove others entirely. Low-branching trees can be "limbed up," which means cutting off the lowest-growing branches. Some trees are more appropriate for limbing up than others. A beech or fir, for example, would be aesthetically undermined if its bottom limbs were pruned away. A yew or apple tree, however, could become even more attractive as more of its glorious, exfoliating bark is exposed through careful limbing up. The removal of any significant tree branches is usually best left to a professional arborist if your pruning experience is limited.

Above: **This healthy planting of ferns, hostas, trillium, and sweet woodruff is the reward for just a bit of care: regular fertilzation, watering, and mulching.**
Right: **Mountain laurel (*Kalmia latifolia*) is an example of a plant that is generally trouble-free when planted in evenly moist, well-drained soil in the shade.**

matter of taste and regional availability, though acid-loving plants can become chlorotic (lose color because of an iron deficiency) if mulched with other than pine or hemlock needles or decayed oak leaves. Leaf mold may be better than shredded mulch on a hill or slope because it is less likely to run in heavy rain. My personal aesthetic preference for a shady setting is pine straw because its smell and feel evoke a woodland sensibility, though straw can become somewhat slippery to walk on. One of my strong horticultural prejudices (I have quite a few but I am trying to keep them to myself) is against those hideous huge nuggets of mulch—I always think when I see them that some immense, lumbering animal has just plodded through the garden and these are the droppings it left behind.

The layer of mulch or leaf mold you put down should be only three or four inches (7 to 10cm) thick and spread evenly around the plantings. Mulch should never be piled heavily right up against the trunks of trees or over the crowns of plants. Too thick a covering of mulch or leaf mold should be avoided because it will encourage mice, voles, and other hungry creatures to settle in for the winter and feed on the roots of your plants.

The time of year you mulch the garden is not really critical and may realistically be a function of when you get around to it. In cold climates it may be preferable to put off mulching in the autumn, when plants are still growing but beginning to slow down, and mulch instead in early winter after the ground has frozen and the plants are assuredly dormant. If you put down a woody mulch during the growing season you should soon thereafter apply a nitrogen-rich fertilizer to the soil; the microorganisms that gradually break down the mulch use nitrogen to do so and thus deplete the nitrogen stored in the soil. How often you need to mulch will be a function of the kind of mulch you use and how thickly you apply it.

PESTS AND DISEASES

A harsh reality of gardening is that we typically learn best how to deal with pests and diseases through first-hand experience. How many of us find it compelling to read about fusarium wilt, botrytis blight, or the feeding habits of slugs until our gardens have been attacked by these nefarious intruders? The primary offensive against plant pests and diseases is thus to take whatever preventive measures we can to erase the need to ever become intimately familiar with these gardening scourges. In practical terms this means adhering as closely as possible to ideal cultural conditions. If a sun-loving plant is grown in shade, for instance, it will be stressed and weakened and clearly more vulnerable to malicious insects and pathogens. Plants grown in a

persistently soggy or incessantly dry garden are likewise threatened unless they are specifically tolerant to such extremes. Excessively fertilized, mulched, or weedy gardens, and those in which the plants are crowded, are all prone to malevolent assault.

Placing the right plants in the right places and following proper cultural practices will assuredly minimize pest and disease problems. Planting a diversity of genera and species will further promote the overall health of your garden. Also include in your design plants that will attract beneficial insects, notably members of the sunflower and parsley families. Most of the plants in these families are sun-loving but several will tolerate light or partial shade, including rudbeckia, green-and-gold, ageratum, and thistle. Impatiens, Dutchman's pipe, abelia, privet, and a great many azaleas will also attract beneficial insects to the shady garden.

Unwanted intruders will inevitably appear from time to time in even the most robust and ecologically well-balanced environment. In addition to being responsible about what, where, and how you plant, you must be vigilant. Look closely at the plants in your garden on a regular basis. Try to notice wilted or distorted buds, leaves that are discolored or chewed, and stems that appear to have been bitten. If you observe anything out of the ordinary, don't ignore it in the naive hope that it will disappear eventually; it probably will not. Consult a good reference book on plant pests and diseases to help you identify the source of

your problem and to get advice for remedial options. For added assurance that you are proceeding properly, consult with your Cooperative Extension Service or a local nurseryman.

Not all plant pests and diseases demand aggressive action. Sometimes cleaning up the garden and removing unwanted weeds and debris will alleviate a mild pest or disease infestation. In some cases you might be able to remove offensive insects by hand, though clearly this works better for relatively large insects like beetles or snails and not at all for tiny and rapidly reproducing insects like aphids or soil-dwellers like root weevils.

Other organic controls include insecticidal soaps, horticultural oils, diatomaceous earth, and microbial insecticides. Their effectiveness will vary depending on the nature and severity of the problem and how often the control is reapplied. Traps can make a dramatic difference in reducing the local groundhog or vole population, especially if the garden is simultaneously opened up enough to allow predatory birds and animals in to help with the job.

In some instances you may decide, after observing and identifying a pest or disease and analyzing the potential remedies, that your best alternative is to do nothing. Perhaps the damage is minimal and can be contained. Maybe the sole cure is ecologically offensive. It may well be, moreover, that a relatively small sacrifice in the short term will lead to a greater gain over time. Remember that the caterpillars chewing on your milkweed leaves may soon become monarch butterflies; grow some extra plants rather than fret about a few leaves.

MAINTENANCE

Proper maintenance of your garden is inextricably tied to proper culture. If your site is well-watered, periodically fertilized, largely free of weeds and debris, not overly congested, and mulched (but not too heavily), then you have gone a long way toward creating a healthy environment. There is no mystery surrounding garden maintenance; it is essentially a matter of experience and common sense. You realize, for instance, that the annuals in your garden will not, by definition, return next spring, so they are best removed entirely if they look unsightly after frost. An exception should made if the plant has persistent seeds that are likely to attract birds through the winter.

Spent perennials should be cut back before new growth begins, though whether you do this in late fall, winter, or early spring is in most cases a matter of personal preference. If your plants remain attractive in the winter or if they entice beneficial wildlife, then by all means leave them standing until early spring. Many ornamental grasses are most striking when their straw- or golden-colored leaves dance and glow in the icy winter winds. Certain plants—caryopteris, butterfly bush, and most herbs—are definitely more likely to survive if their foliage is left intact until spring. If you leave your grasses and perennials standing through the winter, you should, however, clear at least some

spaces and paths in the garden to enable predatory birds and animals to suppress the population of annoying pests that are otherwise likely to settle in for the cold months. It is also a wise idea to cover marginally hardy plants with evergreen branches for added protection. Do this also for any perennials planted late in the fall.

Below: **Variegated hakone grass (*Hakonechloa macra* 'Aureola') is one of the few true grasses that will thrive in the shade (even in quite dry shade). It is, in every respect, an undemanding plant, and requires only that its old foliage be removed before new leaf growth begins in the spring.** *Opposite*: **A mass planting of phlox provides a shot of color beneath a mature shade tree.**

THE AESTHETICS OF GARDENING IN THE SHADE

I recently helped a well-known butterfly expert redesign her garden. She had amassed over the years an impressive collection of host plants and nectar sources and was thus able to attract to her suburban site a remarkable quantity and diversity of butterflies in all stages of development. Her dissatisfaction lay in her realization that she had a collection of plants rather than a beautiful and cohesive garden. Whether you grow vegetables or woodland wildflowers or plants to attract birds and butterflies, the way the garden looks does matter.

How do you know if your garden is aesthetically successful? There are no absolute rules in garden design and what pleases one person may leave someone else unimpressed. My daughter and I were captivated last summer by a courtyard garden in Provincetown, Massachusetts, that consisted of only a few carefully arranged plants and ornaments surrounding a troupe of Barbie and Ken dolls, some in rather bizarre poses. To note that other people looking at this garden were unmoved would be an understatement, but who is to say that humor is not an appropriate element of design?

What you include in your garden and how it is arranged is ultimately a function of personal taste. It would be hard to imagine, however, a greater source of inspiration than nature. This is particularly true for a garden in the shade. A walk through the woods will reveal the artistry, attention to detail, and appreciation of subtlety needed to create a truly engaging garden. A vibrant woodland will show how slight gradations of color, the layering of different sizes and shapes of plants, the use of contrasting and complementary textures, and the interplay of light and shadow can combine to produce a magical effect. Hiking through the woods at different times of the year, you cannot help but notice that one reason why the natural world has such a powerful emotional impact is that it is persistently interesting in an ever-changing way. A healthy forest thus exemplifies certain profound principles of design that can and should be applied to any garden, regardless of size or landscape function.

ENDURING INTEREST

I frequently visit a prominent public garden located not too far from my home. This garden is famous throughout the world for its magnificent collection of plants and its masterful landscaping. I enjoy walking here in winter most of all, when the outlines of the deciduous trees reveal their natural forms and the warm colors of the conifers are so striking against a gray, wintry sky. Winter is not a particularly popular time for visitors, and I usually feel then as if this garden is my own.

In summer, however, the garden is overrun with great swarms of people. The crowds are largest by far where huge beds are planted in expansive sweeps of screamingly bright annuals. To me, these plantings seem too loud and jarring and far too obvious in revealing their charms. At a certain level I also find these beds boring because once planted they do not really change through the growing season, other than becoming taller. In late fall the plants are removed and a vast sea of mulch predominates for the next six months. This is a deeply unsatisfying landscape.

For a garden to be successful it must change, as does the natural world, with the seasons. Something interesting should always be happening. What captures our attention at any one time in a well-designed garden is likely to vary dramatically over the course of days, weeks, or months. In a shade garden in particular there is great potential to create an ever-changing but enduringly enchanting landscape if plants are carefully selected and sited.

Winter is an especially propitious time if you garden in shade. Early-blooming bulbs like snowdrops, winter aconite, and species crocuses will begin to bloom in late January or early February, depending upon the weather. When planted in large drifts, they are a heartening sight on a frigid day, a needed reminder that the garden is still very much alive and spring will indeed come. These early-blooming bulbs are diminutive in nature, and the foliage they leave behind after flowering is relatively inconspicuous, especially if they are planted among herbaceous plants or below deciduous shrubs.

Most perennials that flower very early in the season seem to thrive where they receive winter sun and shade the rest of

the year. Hellebores are generally the first to flower in my garden, typically beginning with the white to pale pink flowers of the Christmas rose (*Helleborus niger*), a native of southern Europe and western Asia with evergreen foliage. The flowers of this and other species of hellebore seem almost perfect when you study them up close—exquisitely cupped or bell-shaped, thoroughly tolerant of frost, and long-lasting when brought in as a cut flower. The flowers of *Helleborus foetidus* (commonly known as "stinking hellebore" because it emits an unpleasant odor when bruised) are chartreuse in color and not as showy as other hellebores, but in terms of form this is a stunning plant. The Lenten rose (*Helleborus orientalis*) has lovely flowers in shades of cream, pale green, and pink and foliage that remains attractive throughout the year, though it may need a bit of tidying up in the spring.

Other shade-loving plants that display striking foliage through the winter (if it is not too severe) include bugleweed, bergenia, and epimedium. Bugleweed (*Ajuga reptans*) has a nasty

Left: **Tommy crocus (*Crocus tomasinianus*) and common snowdrop (*Galanthus nivalis*) are among the first bulbs to bloom, usually beginning to flower in late winter. These little flowers—especially when planted in large drifts—are spectacular examples of the capacity of the garden to raise our spirits.** *Opposite*: **Japanese skimmia (the form shown here is *Skimmia japonica* 'Wisley') is one of the lesser-known broad-leaved evergreens. Its great abundance of cherry red fruit lasts through the winter.**

reputation because it can be invasive and has been known to devour turf. If you grow it in shade in a spot where it cannot take over your lawn, it is a plant of great charm, especially cultivars like 'Jungle Beauty', with its large mahogany-colored leaves, and 'Metallica Crispa', with its tiny burgundy, crinkled foliage. Bergenia (*Bergenia cordifolia*), like bugle-weed, is best grown along a path where you can admire the glorious color of its leaves up close in winter. As the weather turns colder the bold and glossy foliage becomes a stronger shade of burgundy-bronze and remains attractive right up to the emergence of the new green foliage in the spring. The heart-shaped leaves of epimediums, held up above delicate stems, are lighter in color and softer in texture than the bergenias but are no less engaging in glowing shades of orange,

yellow, and red. Epimediums are not well known, possibly because they are so slow-growing when first planted. Once established in a shady site they are quietly beautiful throughout the year. They are tough plants that are able to tolerate light, partial, or full shade, and after several years they will form a lush ground cover.

As you contemplate your garden imagine how delightful it would be to walk outside when snow is still on the ground and see a shrub or small tree with bright yellow blossoms lighting up the dreary winter landscape. Witch hazel, winter jasmine, corylopsis, spicebush, leatherwood, fragrant wintersweet, and cornelian cherry all bloom in late winter, and all are tolerant of light or partial shade. Just one specimen of any of these early-blooming woody plants will enliven your spirits as well as your garden. For best effect they

should be planted where they will be visible from the house and with an evergreen backdrop to set off the sun-colored flowers.

The shady garden seems increasingly vibrant as winter gives way to spring. Brightly colored anemones and blue-flowering glory-of-the-snow (*Chionodoxa* spp.) come into bloom. *Scilla sibirica*, able to grow under trees where nothing else can survive, is tough and free-flowering and a heart-stopping vision when its masses of star-shaped, sky blue flowers appear in early spring. A little later in the season the Spanish bluebells come along in shades of blue, white, and pale pink and combine wonderfully with hostas, ferns, and other perennials, which are perfect for hiding the dying bulb foliage.

Most of the perennials that bloom in the spring flower for only a short period of time. This is fine as long as their

Above: **The scalloped, slightly hairy foliage of lady's mantle (*Alchemilla mollis*) is even more engaging than its bright yellow flowers, especially when drops of dew touch the olive leaves.**
Below: **One of the longest-blooming perennials available, *Corydalis lutea* flowers from spring through autumn.**

foliage remains interesting and attractive throughout the growing season. Alchemilla, Solomon's seal, primroses, crested iris—all of these are engaging long after their flowers have faded. Some spring-blooming perennials for the shade have ephemeral foliage as well as flowers and they have their place in the garden as well, sited carefully so the yellowing foliage is hidden by later-growing plants. Common bleeding-heart (*Dicentra spectabilis*) is one example of such a plant. I could not imagine doing without this old-fashioned beauty but I am careful not to place it in the very front of the garden.

There are only a few shade-tolerant perennials that first bloom in the spring and continue to flower for a long time thereafter. One is corydalis, a plant not taken very seriously until the recent introduction of several new species and cultivars. The easiest form to find is still *Corydalis lutea*, which blooms reliably in my garden from March through November. The foliage is clear green and rather delicate, and the golden yellow racemes dangle on long stalks. Corydalis will flower well in light or partial shade and happily sets seed here and there through the garden, though not in an obnoxious manner. New seedlings are easily removed and passed along to a friend, which is how everyone I know first came upon this plant. A popular new form of corydalis is *C. flexuosa* 'Blue Panda'. It is especially enchanting when planted in a shady rock wall, where its fine foliage and elegant blue flowers can be appreciated up close.

Woody plants that bloom in the shade in spring are generally quite familiar, in some instances perhaps a bit too familiar. There are so many exceptional plants

Above: **The woodland garden in summer, lush and verdant, is the ideal refuge from the season's heat and glaring sunlight.**
Below: **In autumn the shady garden is illuminated by the brightly colored fruits of Japanese skimmia (*Skimmia japonica*).**

that flower at this time of year, even in full shade, that careful selection is a challenge and will very much depend upon the level of shade and space you have in your garden. Since most of us have room for only a few shrubs and small trees, try to focus on plants that will enhance the garden even when not in flower. Several shade-tolerant woodies have intriguing bark, for example—think of the flaky, cinnamon-colored stems of oakleaf hydrangea, the smooth, olive-green branches of Japanese kerria, and the luxuriantly exfoliating bark of the flowering and kousa dogwoods. Other woody plants for the shade have glorious fall foliage or fruit, like skimmia, chokeberry, enkianthus, and numerous different species of viburnum. Still others are notable for their evergreen foliage, and provide the garden with a critical sense of consistent form and structure. Shade-tolerant evergreens include, among others, Prague and leatherleaf viburnums, skimmia, sweet box, taxus, cephalotaxus, osmanthus, fatsia, and a great many rhododendrons and azaleas.

The shady garden in summer is an inviting refuge of cool shades of green, enlivened perhaps by the artful addition of yellow, blue, or variegated foliage plants. There are, to be sure, many plants in full bloom at this time of year in the shade. Hardy amaryllis (*Lycoris squamigera*) only begins to show its graceful, lilac-colored flowers in late summer. Several native lilies bloom in midsummer and perform best in partial shade, including Turk's cap and wood, lemon, and Washington lilies. Daylilies are at their peak in summer and most do appreciate a location outside of the broiling sun,

though in full or dense shade they will not flower well. Other summer-blooming perennials for the shade include kirengeshoma, hardy begonia, obedient plant, thalictrum, and a great range of different species and cultivars of astilbe. Bear in mind that many of the summer-flowering perennials for shade do demand a moist soil and may need supplemental watering. This is true of ligularia, bugbane, lobelia, meadowsweet, queen-of-the-prairie, monkshood, turtlehead, and goatsbeard.

In summer the diversity of annuals able to thrive in the shade becomes evident. Everyone is familiar with impatiens and begonias, but there are so many delightful shady annuals that it would be tragic not to experiment with new genera and species each year. Some prefer the relatively cool weather of late spring and early summer and will languish once it becomes too hot—sweet alyssum, larkspur, pansies, wallflower, and cupflower all bloom best before midsummer in warm climates. Other annuals—usually those native to tropical areas—absolutely flourish in the steamy heat of summer. Coleus, alternanthera, throatwort, and flowering tobacco, to name just a few, fall into this latter category.

As autumn approaches, the shady garden continues to evolve. Autumn bulbs like colchicum, cyclamen, and fall crocuses are in bloom along with such autumn-flowering perennials as toad lily, mist flower, wreath goldenrod, Japanese anemone, and alum root. The foliage of deciduous trees and shrubs and of some herbaceous plants begins to change color with the cooler nights and shortening days. Autumn colors tend not to be

as vibrant in shade as in full sun, but there are shade-tolerant plants that do put on a stunning autumn display. Witch hazel, fothergilla, stewartia, highbush blueberry, viburnum, barberry, and Arkansas amsonia all have spectacular autumn foliage if planted in light or partial shade. Many plants create a dazzling effect, sometimes lasting through the winter, with brightly colored fruits. Think of winterberry, a deciduous holly with startling red berries native to moist areas along woodland edges. Aucuba, mahonia, skimmia, and snowberry also develop showy and persistent fruit, and all but the latter are tolerant of full shade.

With the onset of winter the garden slows down but is by no means quiescent. Common witch hazel (*Hamamelis virginiana*) is hardly commonplace as its clear yellow blossoms light up the December landscape. Camellias are in bloom in southern and western gardens and will continue to flower right through the winter and into spring. Their flowers can be spectacular and the range of colors available is downright dizzying, though I must say I have always found the lack of fragrance in camellias a deep disappointment because they look like they should be sweetly perfumed.

Even when not a flower is in bloom, when the hellebores are still weeks away from delighting us with their elegant blossoms, a thoughtfully designed shade garden will continue to be a source of delight. The unobscured forms of the deciduous trees and shrubs, the colorful trunks and branches of woody plants like stewartia and Japanese dogwood, the haunting sight and sound of the skeletons

25

The contrast of light and shadow enhances the showy flowers of a dogwood tree.

LIGHT AND SHADOW

One of the most alluring aspects of a garden in the shade is the sense of mystery created through the alternating patches of light and dark. As the direction and quality of light changes through the day and through the seasons, it highlights different features of the garden. The enlightened areas appear magical and almost otherworldly. The darkened areas nearby seem like undiscovered treasures, their beauty provocatively hidden until revealed by the light. Depending upon the time of year and the source of shade, this contrast between light and dark, sunlight and shadow, creates an artistic tension in the garden that is almost primordial in its sensuality.

You can enhance the aesthetic impact of light and shadow in your garden through artful pruning and reasonable care in the selection and placement of plants. Prune heavily canopied trees to allow more sunlight to filter through. If your shady site is densely wooded, thin out expendable trees and shrubs. In selecting understory plants remember that light-colored flowers and foliage will be far more prominent in shade than dark-hued ones. Yellow, pale green, light blue, and variegated foliage markedly enliven a shady spot, and white, yellow, or pale pink flowers seem absolutely to glow in the shade. Dark blue and purple flowers seem to get lost when planted in shady areas, especially if seen from a distance. Bright red blossoms like those of the cardinal flower

of spent annuals and perennials left undisturbed for their interesting shapes or to attract wildlife—winter reveals

how an artfully planned garden can indeed be captivating in a dramatically different way throughout the year.

Below: **The dazzling red flowers of the moisture-loving cardinal flower (*Lobelia cardinalis*) will stand out even in relatively deep shade.**
Bottom: **Pale flowers, like these white and blush-tinted impatiens, take on a luminous quality when planted in shade. Impatiens flower freely even in deep shade, and have become one of the best-loved garden plants.**

alba 'Elegantissima' will, if planted in a dark corner, draw your eye to that spot in a most engaging manner.

Variegated foliage is not always easy to integrate into the garden and a few words of caution may be helpful. If you mix differently colored variegated plants in the same section of the garden, it will surely look busy and cluttered. Using a range of different kinds of variegated plants in a small area, even if they all have the same color theme, can also be disorienting. The point is that variegated foliage should be used in moderation and the accompanying plants should complement rather than compete with the variegated ones. One of my favorite hostas, for example, is a cultivar called 'Patriot' with forest green leaves striped irregularly in clear white. I might combine this with white impatiens for a simple yet elegant composition, or with *Anemone* x *hybrida* 'Alba' or some other late, white-flowering perennial. The more complicated you get when designing with variegated foliage, the more likely you are to run into trouble; keep it simple.

In a shady garden you really must try to take full advantage of the available light. Thoughtful pruning and thinning, the creative use of plants with light-colored leaves and flowers, and the prudent integration of variegated plants will all brighten a shady environment. Where you place your plants can also make a difference. Notice how some plants seem luminescent if they are sited where backlit by either the early morning or late afternoon sun. This will make the garden appear to be, at least at certain times of the day, distinctly more vibrant and alive.

(*Lobelia cardinalis*) leap out and demand your attention.

Variegated foliage never seems to work in full sun. Bright sunlight makes such plants appear drab and colorless. In deep shade, on the other hand, plants with multicolored leaves can be electri-

fying. A clump of variegated hakone grass (*Hakonechloa macra* 'Aureola') on a shady slope or overhanging a sunless section of a rock wall, for example, will thoroughly illuminate that part of the garden. The white-margined specimen of red-twig dogwood known as *Cornus*

COLOR

One of the first things you notice in a successful shade garden is the subtle use of color. There will, of course, be patches of exuberantly tinted flowers or foliage—imagine the fiery orange-red flowers of the torch azalea (*Rhododendron kaempferi*), the buttery yellow blossoms of ligularia, or the golden leaves of Bowles golden sedge—but they are used sparingly and in harmony with the predominant green of the surrounding plants. Shade gardens are, almost by definition, places of rest and repose. The colors we use and the ways in which they are combined should enhance this sense of tranquility.

The value of green foliage in a shady site is immense. Green-leaved plants evoke the sensibility of a quiet woodland. They create an aura of peacefulness that transcends the ephemeral beauty of even the loveliest flowers. There are so many different shades of green—from the deep, forest green of Christmas fern to the bluish green of 'Blue Mist' fothergilla to the pale chartreuse of hayscented fern—that you could easily create a garden just of green-leaved plants and never find it monotonous.

Gray-leaved plants are as beautiful as they are useful in the garden. Their soft neutrality serves as a unifying force, pulling together difficult colors and enhancing the overall sense of equanimity and cohesiveness. With the notable exceptions of Japanese painted fern and several cultivars of lamium, however, there are few plants with silvery foliage that are able to tolerate shade. A potential alternative in light or partial shade may be some of the blue-leaved hosta cultivars. There are many of these available today, with a wide range of foliage sizes and shapes. *Hosta sieboldiana* 'Elegans' is probably still the most popular, but other cultivars worth trying include 'Blue Moon', 'Blue Umbrellas', and 'Halcyon'. Any of these cultivars would, if planted in drifts, be most welcome in the garden in both practical and aesthetic terms.

Below: **In midsummer the startling yellow flowers of rocket ligularia (*Ligularia stenocephala* 'The Rocket') contrast sharply with the plant's blackish purple stems.** *Bottom*: **These hot-colored primroses happily grow in light shade.** *Opposite*: **The long, narrow leaves of Japanese iris provide a critical vertical element to the garden, compelling one to look up toward the trees.**

TEXTURE AND FORM

I spent a great deal of time last summer trying to figure out why a garden I maintain was not working well. There was something definitely amiss and it nagged at me relentlessly until one day the answer appeared with blinding clarity. There were, to put it simply, too many plants with roundish leaves. There was a large variety of plants here to be sure—there were roses, butterfly bushes, and all sorts of different annuals and perennials—but there was a sameness of form and texture that caused the whole picture to seem rather boring. The flowers were exquisite and the plants were impeccably maintained, but the lack of contrast in this garden created an inescapable sense of tedium.

A garden must include enough plants with different shapes and textures to sustain interest over a long period of time. It need not, indeed it should not, be a hodgepodge where each plant is dramatically unlike the neighboring one. That would be aesthetically agitating to the extreme. But there should be at least some carefully considered distinctions between the different groupings of plants. The abovementioned garden was transformed by removing a few roses and putting in their place several clumps of Siberian irises. The vertical leaves of the irises made a compelling difference because of their stark contrast with surrounding plants. Their long, linear foliage also forced the eye upward, and the garden suddenly appeared lighter and more ethereal.

There are infinite possibilities in a shady garden to artfully combine plants with varying textures and shapes. A hedge of horizontally shaped catawba rhododendrons with shiny, elongated leaves and relatively horizontal form is captivating when underplanted with the finely whorled foliage of sweet woodruff. This would be a pleasing composition long before and after their respective flowers had come and gone. The feathery texture of astilbe, as another example, would be even more pronounced if planted alongside a group of large-leaved hostas like 'Krossa Regal' or in front of a relatively coarse plant like rodgersia or a spiky one like Japanese iris. A massing of northern maidenhair fern, with its graceful and lacy foliage, would be splendid beside a

groundcover planting of the glossy, oval-leaved European wild ginger.

Whatever combinations you pursue will naturally depend upon your site and personal preferences. Try to avoid too many contrasts in a small area because the effect will be disquieting. Bear in mind, however, that a garden without some dissimilar forms and textures, without some distinctly different leaf and plant shapes, will inevitably seem flat and uninspired.

LAYERING

In a healthy and horticulturally diverse woodland one of the first things you may notice, consciously or not, is an aura of luxuriant depth. The landscape seems palpably lush. Even in the dead of winter there is a clear sense of being in the midst of a living, ecologically exuberant environment. To a great extent this sensibility emanates from the layering of plants typically found in a forest setting. The specific character of the different layers will vary widely by region and from site to site and is likely to be a result and reflection of the evolution of that particular land. When it was last cleared and for what purpose, to what extent it has since been allowed to function without human intererence, what kinds of wildlife are at home here and in what quantities—these are just a few of the many factors that determine the content and well-being of a contemporary forest.

In a forest the largest evergreen and deciduous trees tower above the subsequent layer of medium- and small-size trees, big shrubs, and tall perennials. This layer is in turn underplanted with smaller woody plants and other herbaceous perennials and annuals. At the lowest level are those woody and herbaceous plants that grow low to the ground and mosses that hug the forest floor. This is of course a simplified approximation of the structure of a woodland but is useful nonetheless as a guide to building layer by layer a richly planted and well-designed shady garden.

If you garden in the shade, the upper canopy of your garden is probably predetermined. It may, for example, be a mature oak or maple or a large specimen or group of conifers. It might be the tall building right up alongside your garden. What is left for you to design will in most cases be the middle and lower levels. There are many woody and herbaceous plants appropriate for these understory layers, though they vary somewhat depending upon your specific cultural conditions, site, climate, and intensity of shade.

A low-maintenance alternative to mulching under shrubs is to use bold perennials like hosta (*Hosta sieboldianna* is shown here) as a deciduous groundcover. Early spring bulbs can be planted behind the hostas, for when the bulbs finish flowering the hostas will grow and cover the unsightly bulb foliage.

Study woodland landscapes in your area and observe the kinds of understory plants that grow there. Examine where and how they grow and the kinds of plants with which they might naturally combine. You might notice, for instance, that a shadbush is perfectly content beneath a large oak tree. Below the shadbush colonies of ostrich fern, Jack-in-the-pulpit, mayapple, and dog-tooth violets might well have settled in to form a thoroughly harmonious, everchanging composition. Borrow specific and conceptual design ideas freely from those woodland settings that are most aesthetically pleasing to you and most appropriate to your individual site. As you analyze the multi-level complexity of a healthy forest, just remember that this took a great many years to accomplish and recall that, along with enthusiasm, curiosity, and attention to detail, patience is a virtue shared by every successful gardener.

Above: **A mass planting of wild blue phlox (***Phlox divaricata***) is eye-catching in early spring when few other perennials have yet begun to flower.** *Right*: **An underplanting of ferns perfectly complements the double-flowered dogwood and creates a scene of lush refinement.**

DECIDUOUS UNDERSTORY TREES

Cornus alternifolia

Acer pensylvanicum

COMMON NAMES:
STRIPED MAPLE, MOOSEWOOD,
WHISTLEWOOD

Family: Aceraceae
Hardiness: To Zone 3
Shade Tolerance/Preference: Partial to full shade

Habit and Mature Size: Striped maple is a small tree or large shrub that grows to 20 feet (6m) (may be up to 30 feet [9m] in the wild); it is usually somewhat less broad than tall with an uneven crown.

Aesthetic Value: This tree is notable for its smooth, bright green bark with white longitudinal stripes. The autumn foliage of the striped maple is lemon yellow.

Acer pensylvanicum

Cultural Needs: Striped maple requires well-drained, moist, slightly acidic soil in relatively cool conditions. It should be protected from sun and wind, and it is best to plant this tree balled and burlapped in early spring.

Landscape Uses: Use striped maple as an understory tree at the edge of a shady setting. Songbirds, upland ground birds, and small mammals are all attracted to this tree.

Insects and Diseases: Striped maple has no significant problems if well-sited.

Cultivars: 'Erythrocladum' has young stems that are bright red in winter.

Amelanchier arborea

COMMON NAMES:
DOWNY SERVICEBERRY,
JUNEBERRY, SHADBUSH

Family: Rosaceae
Hardiness: Zones 4–9
Shade Tolerance/Preference: Partial shade or full sun

Habit and Mature Size: Typically a single-stem plant with a rounded crown at maturity, downy serviceberry ultimately grows 15 to 25 feet (4.6 to 7.5m) tall and as wide.

Aesthetic Value: Lovely white flowers in pendulous clusters bloom in mid to late April. The flowers are ephemeral but act as a wonderful harbinger of spring. The bark is smoky gray in color and smooth but for handsome vertical fissures that become even more pronounced with age. The alternate leaves turn yellow to apricot in the fall and the fruit changes from green to red to blackish purple as it ripens.

Cultural Needs: Downy serviceberry should be transplanted balled and burlapped. It grows best in moist, well-drained acidic soil; this plant is not tolerant of pollution.

Landscape Uses: Effective at the edge of woods in a naturalistic setting, downy serviceberry looks especially beautiful alongside a stream or pond. Its sweet berries ripen in June and attract birds to the garden, and its bark is most appealing in winter.

Insects and Diseases: Rust, leaf blight, fire blight, powdery mildew, leaf miner, borers, Japanese beetles, and lacebugs are possible but infrequent pests.

Amelanchier arborea

Amelanchier laevis

Other species: *Amelanchier laevis* (Allegheny serviceberry) is very much like its cousin, *A. arborea* (downy serviceberry), but the new leaves of *A. laevis* have a bronze cast. The clear white flowers appear, as with *A. arborea*, before the leaves emerge in spring. Zones 4–8.

Cercis canadensis

COMMON NAME:

EASTERN REDBUD

Family: Leguminosae
Hardiness: Zones 4–9
Shade Tolerance/Preference: Light to partial shade

Habit and Mature Size: The eastern redbud grows 20 to 30 feet (6 to 9m) tall and 25 to 35 feet (7.5 to 11m) wide. Habit is spreading, and the crown is usually flat-topped; growth is generally multistemmed and low-branching. Young twigs form a zigzag pattern.

Aesthetic Value: Reddish purple buds open in April to pale rose-colored flowers. Flowers are long-lasting and appear before the leaves. The fruit is a 2- to 3-foot (61 to 91.5cm) long pod and often persists through the winter. The leaves are heart-shaped and turn a golden yellow in autumn.

Cultural Needs: The eastern redbud prefers somewhat moist, well-drained soil but will tolerate dry conditions. It is best to transplant when the tree is still small. Regular watering and fertilization will ensure sustained vigor.

Landscape Uses: The vibrant pink flowers of redbud are wonderful when seen against an evergreen background. It can be used in a shrub border or woodland garden and is effective as a single specimen or in groups.

Insects and Diseases: Canker may cause stems to die back. Other potential problems are verticillium wilt, leaf spots, tree hoppers, and scales.

Cultivars: The eastern redbud has several popular culitivars: 'Alba' has white flowers; 'Withers Pink Charm' has pink flowers without the purple tint of the species; 'Silver Cloud' has green leaves with creamy-white splotches; 'Forest Pansy' has brilliant reddish purple foliage, especially when the new leaves emerge, but is not hardy below −10°F (−24°C).

Cercis canadensis

Clethra barbinervis

COMMON NAME:

JAPANESE CLETHRA

Family: Clethraceae
Hardiness: Zones 5–8
Shade Tolerance/Preferance: Partial to light shade

Habit and Mature Size: Japanese clethra can be a multistemmed shrub or a single-stem tree. It grows 15 to 20 feet (4.6 to 6m) tall and about 8 feet (2.4m) wide.

Aesthetic Value: Japanese clethra flowers in late summer. The fragrant, white flowers form long clusters. The bark exfoliates in shades of brown, beige, and orange and is more and more spectacular as the tree matures. Autumn foliage color is rather uninteresting.

Cultural Needs: Flourishing in acidic, moist, well-drained soil, Japanese clethra may need supplemental watering in dry weather.

Clethra barbinervis

35

Landscape Uses: Japanese clethra is excellent as a specimen in a shrub border or mixed border because it flowers later than other woody plants and its bark is glorious in the winter.

Insects and Diseases: Spider mites may infect Japanese clethra in very dry conditions.

Cornus kousa

COMMON NAMES:
KOUSA DOGWOOD,
JAPANESE FLOWERING DOGWOOD

Family: Cornaceae
Hardiness: Zones 5–8
Shade Tolerance/Preference: Partial shade or full sun

Habit and Mature Size: Kousa dogwood grows about 20 to 25 feet (6 to 7.5m) tall and equally wide. It is quite upright, almost vase-shaped when young but grows rounder and more horizontal with age.

Aesthetic Value: Kousa dogwood's true flowers are inconspicuous but its bracts are large and pointed and last for several weeks. The bracts are white at the outset but turn a pale pink over time. The fruit is bright red and resembles a large raspberry. Foliage turns lovely shades of scarlet and burnt orange in the fall and the bark exfoliates in patches of gray, tan, and deep brown.

Cultural Needs: Kousa dogwood performs best in acidic, well-drained, sandy soil with organic material added. It should be transplanted balled and burlapped and planted as a young specimen. Limb up the lowest branches when the tree is young so the exfoliating trunk is shown to best advantage as it matures.

Landscape Uses: This tree is attractive throughout the year, and seems to be more drought-, pest-, and insect-resistant than its popular cousin *C. florida*. It is ideal as a single specimen or when planted in groups, and its horizontal form and multicolored bark are very much appreciated in the winter landscape.

Insects and Diseases: Kuosa dogwood does not seem as vulnerable to anthracnose or to the other pests and diseases that plague *C. florida*.

Cultivars: 'Chinensis' has particularly large and long-lasting white bracts; 'Satomi' (syn. 'Rosabella') has bright pink bracts; 'Summer Stars' is the latest and longest to bloom, sometimes still flowering into late summer as the fruits develop. The autumn color is superb and the ultimate height of this cultivar is 18 to 20 feet (5.5 to 6m).

Other Species: *Cornus alternifolia* (pagoda dogwood). The yellowish white flowers in spring are not particularly ornamental, but this plant is valuable nevertheless for its unusual horizontal form and the reddish or purplish brown color of its stems in winter. The fruit changes from green to red to bluish black. Fruit stalks are pinkish red in color and persistent. This is the only dogwood with alternate leaves. Zones 3–7.

Cornus kousa

Cornus florida (flowering dogwood) has showy white bracts that appear in spring (the true flowers are small, greenish white, and insignificant), lush green foliage turns wine red in autumn, cherry red fruit is attractive and appealing to birds, and bark is grayish and interestingly blocky, especially on older specimens. Zones 5–9

Cornus mas (Cornelian cherry) is one of the first trees to flower in spring—its clear yellow blossoms appear in March, before the tree has leafed out, and usually last for about three weeks. The fruit is a bright red drupe (a stone fruit, like a peach or a cherry), though it is often hidden by the dense foliage. The bark, which is shaggy and exfoliates in patches of gray and brown, is very appealing in winter. Zones 4–8, though less vigorous in warm climates.

Halesia carolina

COMMON NAME: CAROLINA SILVERBELL

Family: Styracaceae

Hardiness: Zones 5–8

Shade Tolerance/Preference:
Partial or light shade to full sun

Habit and Mature Size: Carolina silverbell may grow either as a rather narrow tree with ascending branches or with more horizontal branching and a rounder overall form. Its mature height is 30 to 40 feet (9 to 12m) and the ultimate spread is 20 to 30 feet (6 to 9m).

37

Cornus mas

Halesia carolina

Aesthetic Value: This tree has graceful, pendulous clusters of white, bell-shaped flowers in spring. The flowers are ephemeral, usually lasting only about one week, but are nonetheless charming in a quiet way. The bark is grayish with wide, pale ridges. The bark on two-year-old twigs peels in fine threads.

Cultural Needs: Carolina silverbell prefers a rich, moist, acidic soil and may become chlorotic (the green parts of the plant may appear blanched) in soil with a high pH. Transplant this tree balled and burlapped in early spring.

Landscape Uses: Use Carolina silverbell as a specimen tree close to or right up alongside a house or patio, where its delicate flowers can best be viewed and appreciated. It has deep roots and is thus easily underplanted with lower-growing woody plants or perennials.

Insects and Diseases: This tree has no serious pests or diseases.

Cultivars: 'Rosea' has pink flowers that are attractive to hummingbirds.

Stewartia pseudocamellia

COMMON NAME: JAPANESE STEWARTIA

Family: Theaceae

Hardiness: Zones 5–8

Shade Tolerance/Preference:
Morning sun and light shade in the afternoon is ideal.

Habit and Mature Size: This is a pyramidal to oval tree that grows about 35 feet (11m) tall in a garden setting and close to 60 feet (18m) in the wild. Its mature width is about 20 feet (7.5m).

Aesthetic Value: This is one of the best small ornamental trees available. It has white, camellialike flowers with bright yellow stamens in summer and spectacular foliage in autumn. Most impressive is the multicolored exfoliating bark, a veritable patchwork of varying shades of orange, brown, pale gray, and reddish brown.

Cultural Needs: Japanese stewartia likes a soil rich in organic matter, neither too wet nor too dry, and on the

Stewartia pseudocamellia

acidic side. If grown in full sun in a warm climate, the leaf margins will tend to burn. It is best to plant this tree in early spring; it may take some time to recover from transplanting. Japanese stewartia is slow-growing.

Landscape Uses: Japanese stewartia is excellent as a specimen tree or when planted in groups along the edge of a woodland garden. This is a magnificent tree throughout the year, especially as it ages, and it should be sited in a prominent location.

Insects and Diseases: Japanese stewartia is not affected by serious pests or diseases.

Viburnum prunifolium

COMMON NAME: BLACKHAW VIBURNUM

Family: Caprifoliaceae
Hardiness: Zones 3–9
Shade Tolerance/Preference: Sun or shade

Habit and Mature Size: Blackhaw viburnum tends to be a multistemmed, rather coarse tree with a roundish crown. It grows 15 to 20 feet (4.6 to 6m) tall and 10 to 12 feet (3 to 3.7m) wide.

Aesthetic Value: Blackhaw viburnum has white, flat-topped flower clusters with red petals and yellow stamens. Flowers appear in early May and are followed by rose-colored fruits that turn bluish black as they ripen. Handsome green leaves turn shades of red and bronze in autumn. The leaves look very much like cherry leaves but grow opposite each other on the stem rather than alternating up the stem.

Cultural Needs: This tree is very tough and adaptable to different soil types, even very dry soil. Suckers should be cut to the ground when they appear.

Landscape Uses: Its small size, resilience, and multiseason interest make this a good choice for an urban garden or any site where space is limited and cultural conditions are less than ideal. The fruit is edible and has been used for preserves since colonial days. It is also very appealing to birds.

Insects and Diseases: This tree has no serious pests or diseases.

Viburnum prunifolium

SHADE-
TOLERANT
EVERGREEN
TREES

Cryptomeria japonica

Chamaecyparis nootkatensis

COMMON NAME:
NOOTKA FALSE CYPRESS

Family: Cupressaceae
Hardiness: Zones 4–7
Shade Tolerance/Preference: Sun or light to partial shade

Habit and Mature Size: This tree grows 60 feet (18m) tall and 20 feet (6m) wide in a narrowly pyramidal shape. The rate of growth is approximately 12 inches (30.5cm) per year.

Aesthetic Value: Dark, lush green foliage and stately form make this a particularly handsome plant. The leaves have a rank odor when rubbed or bruised.

Chamaecyparis nootkatensis

Cultural Needs: Nootka false cypress will thrive where there is ample moisture and good drainage. It is also able to tolerate wind, unlike most other species of false cypress.

Landscape Uses: Nootka false cypress makes an excellent screen when planted in groups and is a good alternative to the more insect-prone hemlock. It is also effective when planted as a single specimen.

Insects and Diseases: Bagworms are sometimes a problem.

Cultivars: 'Pendula' has drooping branches and is somewhat shorter than the species.

Cryptomeria japonica

COMMON NAME:
JAPANESE CEDAR

Family: Taxodiaceae
Hardiness: Zones 6–9
Shade Tolerance/Preference: Sun or light shade

Habit and Mature Size: Japanese cedar is a graceful, pyramidal tree that grows 60 to 70 feet (18 to 21m) tall and 25 feet (7.5) wide. It has wide-spreading branches and a relatively stout trunk.

Aesthetic Value: Bluish green foliage, refined habit, and reddish brown exfoliating bark combine to great effect. In some areas the foliage may have a tendency to become brown, in which case one of its cultivars would be a better choice.

Cultural Needs: Japanese cedar grows best in a rich but not overly dense acidic soil with adequate moisture. Plant it in a site protected from strong winds.

Landscape Uses: This is one of the best conifers for a southern garden. It makes a lovely specimen tree or a beautiful grove when planted in groups.

Insects and Diseases: Leaf blight, leaf spot, and spider mites may all present problems.

Cultivars: 'Elegans' grows 9 to 15 feet (2.6 to 4.6m) tall and has feathery, soft green foliage that turns brownish red in winter; 'Elegans Nana' grows only 3 feet (1m) tall and 7 feet (2m) wide. It is densely branched and bushy in habit with bluish green foliage that turns bronze in winter; 'Yoshino' is one of the very best cultivars of Japanese cedar. It has a narrow, somewhat pyramidal habit and it is hardier and holds its lower branches better than the species.

Thuja occidentalis

COMMON NAMES:
AMERICAN ARBORVITAE, EASTERN ARBORVITAE, WHITE CEDAR

Family: Cupressaceae
Hardiness: Zones 2–7
Shade Tolerance/Preferance:
Sun or partial to light shade

Habit and Mature Size: American arborvitae is a narrow, pyramidal tree that grows 40 feet (21m) tall and 15 feet (4.6m) wide.

Aesthetic Value: American arborvitae has dense, flat green foliage that can become somewhat yellow or brown in winter. The bark is reddish to grayish brown and rather attractive, though it is usually not noticed because this tree branches to the ground.

Cultural Needs: This tree requires a deep, well-drained soil with adequate moisture. Do not use in overly dry areas or where it is likely to be exposed to wind, snow, or ice damage. It can be transplanted any time of year.

Landscape Uses: This is an overused but nonetheless effective hedge or foundation plant. Its vertical form and habit of branching right down to the ground make it a useful screen or windbreak. If you plan to plant American arborvitae in a prominent spot, be sure to choose a cultivar that has good foliage color throughout the year. It is difficult to underplant American arborvitae because its roots are shallow and widespreading.

Insects and Diseases: Bagworms, spider mites, and deer may all affect this tree.

Cultivars: 'Emerald' grows 6 feet (1.8m) tall but only 2 feet (61cm) wide and makes a lush hedge planted in groups. 'Hetz Midget' is a dwarf, globe-shaped form. It

has lustrous foliage and matures at 3 to 4 feet (1 to 1.2m) tall and 4 feet (1.2m) wide; it is striking in a rock garden. 'Nigra' has a narrow form and its foliage stays green in winter. 'Techny' is slightly wider than Nigra and its foliage has a bluish cast. This is one of the best cultivars for northern gardens because its foliage remains attractive year-round.

Other species: *Thuja plicata* has thicker, darker green foliage than American arborvitae and tends to hold its color better in winter. Zones 5–7.

Thuja occidentalis

Thujopsis dolabrata

COMMON NAMES:

HIBA ARBORVITAE, FALSE ARBORVITAE

Family: Cupressaceae

Hardiness: Zones 5–7

Shade Tolerance/Preference:

Light or partial shade or full sun

Habit and Mature Size: This is a dense, pyramidal tree that grows 30 to 50 feet (9 to 12m) tall and about 15 feet (4.6m) wide.

Aesthetic Value: The leaves of hiba arborvitae are bright green and the underside has patches of white. The texture is rather coarse.

Cultural Needs: Hiba arborvitae prefers moist, acidic soil rich in organic material and protection from intense winds.

Landscape Uses: While this plant is not easy to find, it is an impressive evergreen with an interesting texture. It is a good alternative to the overplanted American arborvitae and may well be more shade-tolerant.

Insects and Diseases: Hiba arborvitae has no serious pests or diseases.

Cultivars: 'Nana' has a rounded form and grows about 3 feet (1m) high.

Tsuga canadensis

COMMON NAMES:

CANADIAN HEMLOCK, EASTERN HEMLOCK

Family: Pinaceae

Hardiness: Zones 3–7

Shade Tolerance/Preference: Light, partial, or full shade

Habit and Mature Size: This is a broadly conical tree that spreads 35 to 50 feet (11 to 15m) wide and reaches an ultimate height of 70 to 80 feet (21 to 24m). It has a very dense habit and its branches droop gracefully at the tips as the tree matures. Canadian hemlock may be multistemmed or single-stemmed; in any event the central leader is always pendulous.

Aesthetic Value: A healthy specimen of Canadian hemlock is exceptionally beautiful. It is elegant in form and texture, its foliage is a dark and glossy green throughout the year, its bark is an attractive charcoal gray, and it has small, ornamental cones.

Cultural Needs: Canadian hemlock prefers a cool climate and rich, moist, acidic soil. It does not react well to pollution, poor drainage, drought, or strong winds. It is best to transplant this tree balled and burlapped in early spring.

Landscape Uses: This can be a wonderful evergreen screen or hedge if kept free of pests and disease. It reacts well to pruning, especially if only the individual shoots are removed every year rather than shearing the entire plant. Avoid underplanting because Canadian hemlock has shallow, fibrous, and wide-spreading roots.

Insects and Diseases: Woolly adelgid has been a terrible problem in the Northeast in recent years. Scale, leaf blight, cankers, blister rust, hemlock borer, spider mites, bagworm, and gypsy moth are but a few of the pests and diseases that plague Canadian hemlock.

Other Species: *Tsuga caroliniana* has foliage that is glossy green on leaf tops and pale green on the underside. The foliage radiates around the stem to create a whorled effect. Bark is reddish brown and develops deep fissures over time.

Tsuga canadensis

43

DECIDUOUS
SHRUBS

Abelia x grandiflora

Abelia × grandiflora

COMMON NAME:

GLOSSY ABELIA

Family: Caprifoliaceae

Hardiness: Zones 6–9

Shade Tolerance/Preference: Full sun to partial shade

Habit and Mature Size: Glossy abelia grows as a spreading, multistemmed shrub with arching branches. It grows to about 3 to 6 feet (1 to 1.8m) high and about as wide, though it may be smaller in colder climates if it dies back in the winter. It has a graceful, rather open habit.

Aesthetic Value: Throughout the summer and into the autumn, this plant is covered in small, whitish pink, funnel-shaped flowers. The flowers are mildly fragrant. Leaves are finely textured and glossy green in summer and purplish bronze in the fall; if winter is not too severe the foliage may persist through the cold weather. New stems are reddish brown and the older ones exfoliate to reveal the lighter inner bark.

Cultural Needs: Glossy abelia prefers a well-drained, acidic soil and requires careful siting if grown in a cool climate. Any pruning and removal of deadwood should be done in early spring—the plant blooms on new wood.

Landscape Uses: This is a superb choice for massing, for slope stabilization, or in the shrub or mixed border. In southern gardens, where there is no danger of winter dieback, glossy abelia makes an excellent evergreen hedge. It blooms when most other shrubs have finished flowering and over a remarkably long period of time. The glossy leaves of this shrub are shown to best advantage when it is combined with the matte green of broad-leaved or needled evergreens. Glossy abelia also attracts butterflies, especially swallowtails, to the garden.

Insects and Diseases: Glossy abelia has no serious pests or diseases.

Cultivars: 'Prostrata' is a lower-growing, more compact form with white flowers. It makes a good groundcover in areas where it is reliable hardy. 'Sherwood' is more dense than the species and the leaves are smaller and more delicate.

Aesculus parviflora

COMMON NAME:

BOTTLEBRUSH BUCKEYE

Family: Hippocastanaceae

Hardiness: Zones 5–8

Shade Tolerance/Preference:

Prefers partial shade but will tolerate full sun if not too dry

Habit and Mature Size: This is a plant that becomes quite wide-spreading over time and suckers heavily. It is multistemmed with slender branches. The lower branches are horizontal and lie almost on the ground, while the upper branches are attractively ascending. It is slow-growing but over time will become 8 to 12 feet (2.4 to 3.7m) tall and about twice as wide.

Aesculus parviflora

45

Aesthetic Value: Bottlebrush buckeye blooms in July, when few other shrubs are in flower. It has large, upright, candlelike, white flower spikes that are prominent even from a great distance. The flowers persist for a few weeks and are slightly fragrant and very appealing to insects. The leaves are bold and coarse and palmately compound in shape. They turn a nice yellow in autumn, though they drop off quickly. The intriguing stems and large terminal buds make this an interesting plant in the winter.

Cultural Needs: A rich, moist soil on the acidic side is ideal. This shrub can be transplanted either balled and burlapped or from a container in early spring but does sometimes take a while to recover from transplanting.

Landscape Uses: Bottlebrush buckeye will form a dense thicket in time and should be given enough space to do so. It is one of the few shrubs that looks wonderful planted in a group in the middle of a lawn. Even when not in bloom, its coarse foliage and strong stems draw your attention. It is also effective if allowed to naturalize on the edge of a woodland or when planted as an understory hedge beneath shade trees.

Insects and Diseases: Bottlebrush buckeye has no serious pests or diseases.

Cultivars: 'Roger's' flowers later than the species and its inflorescences are distinctly longer.

Aronia arbutifolia

COMMON NAME:
RED CHOKEBERRY

Family: Rosaceae
Hardiness: Zones 5–9
Shade Tolerance/Preference:
Sun or light shade

Habit and Mature Size: Red chokeberry spreads by underground suckers and grows 6 to 8 feet (1.8 to 2.4m) tall and 3 to 5 feet (1 to 1.5m) wide. It has an open, fountainlike form with slender, arching branches.

Aesthetic Value: The white flowers of red chokeberry are not terribly ornamental. The leaves, however, are a deep, shiny geen in summer and a brilliant crimson in autumn.

The fruit, especially on the cultivar 'Brilliantissima', is bright red and often persists until late winter.

Cultural Needs: Red chokeberry is tolerant of different kinds of soil conditions. Thin old growth in early spring to ensure good air circulation. On older plants leaves tend to be concentrated on the upper half of the plant so it might be wise to use a lower plant in the foreground to hide the bare stems.

Landscape Uses: This is a good plant for a site along the edge of a woodland garden, especially in combination with dark green evergreens. It is also attractive when planted in groups in a shrub border. The fruit is too bitter for humans but is appealing to birds.

Insects and Diseases: Red chokeberry suffers from no serious pests or diseases.

Cultivars: 'Brilliantissima' has more fruit and it is glossier and deeper red in color than the species; its autumn foliage is outstanding. 'Erecta' has a narrow, vertical habit.

Clethra alnifolia

COMMON NAMES:
SWEET PEPPERBUSH, SUMMERSWEET CLETHRA

Family: Clethraceae
Hardiness: Zones 4–9
Shade Tolerance/Preference:
Light or partial shade

Habit and Mature Size: Sweet pepperbush is an oval-shaped and round-topped shrub which suckers to form groves. Each plant grows about 5 to 8 feet (1.5 to 2.4m) in height and 6 to 8 feet (1.8 to 1.4m) in width. The habit is upright and erect and plants tend to be multistemmed.

Aesthetic Value: The leaves of sweet pepperbush are deep green in summer and turn a clear yellow in fall. Flowers appear in summer—they are white, borne on short stalks, extremely fragrant, and of great delight to bees. The fruit is a dry capsule that persists through the winter and is mildly ornamental.

Cultural Needs: Sweet pepperbush is native to wet areas and will thus grow best where the soil is reliably

Clethra alnifolia

moist. It also prefers that the soil be on the acidic side. It is very tolerant of salt spray and compacted soil. Supplemental watering is advisable during droughts.

Landscape Uses: Its habit of spreading laterally and its need for moist soil makes this an ideal plant for naturalizing alongside a pond or stream. It is native to and perfectly suited for a seashore setting. It is also an excellent choice for attracting skippers, swallowtails, and other butterflies to the garden.

Insects and Diseases: Sweet pepperbush has no serious pests if it is well-sited.

Cultivars: 'Hummingbird' is a dwarf form from Calloway Gardens in Georgia. It is attractively compact and bushy, growing only 2 or 3 feet (61cm to 1m) tall. 'Rosea' has pink flower buds and pink flowers and in habit and form is similar to the species.

Cornus alba *'Elegantissima'* (a.k.a. *'Argenteo-marginata'*)

COMMON NAME:
VARIEGATED TATARIAN DOGWOOD

Family: Cornaceae / **Hardiness:** Zones 2–7
Shade Tolerance/Preference: Full sun or light shade

Habit and Mature Size: This multistemmed plant grows approximately 8 to 10 feet (2.4 to 3m) tall and wide; the spread may be greater because of suckering. The habit is mounded in youth and arching as the plant ages.

Aesthetic Value: This particular cultivar is known for its leaves, which are bright green with a creamy white margin. Like the species, the stems are bright red in winter, especially if grown in full sun. The flowers are yellowish white and not particularly showy.

Cultural Needs: Variegated Tatarian dogwood prefers a moist, well-drained soil. If grown in full sun, the stem color will be most vibrant, but the foliage may suffer. The variegated foliage will hold up better in light shade, though the tradeoff is that the winter stems will not be as colorful. Once the plant is well-established, prune out one third of the old growth early in the spring each year because the winter color is best on the new stems.

Cornus alba *'Elegantissima'*

47

Landscape Uses: A mass planting of variegated Tatarian dogwood in a shrub border or alongside a pond is very ornamental throughout the year. A single specimen is also effective as a foundation plant, in a mixed border, or in a city garden where space is limited.

Insects and Diseases: Scale and borers may affect variegated Tatarian dogwood.

Corylopsis pauciflora

COMMON NAME:
BUTTERCUP WINTER HAZEL

Family: Hamamelidaceae
Hardiness: Zones 6–8
Shade Tolerance/Preference: Light or partial shade

Habit and Mature Size: The ultimate height of buttercup winter hazel is 4 to 6 feet (1.2 to 1.8m) tall. The spread is equal to or greater than the height. In texture and form this is a delicate shrub.

Corylopsis pauciflora

Aesthetic Value: In early spring, before the leaves emerge, pale yellow pendulous flower clusters appear. The flowers are fragrant and ideal for indoor forcing. Leaves are a clear green and heart-shaped. The stems are thin and have a wiry branching habit that evokes a sense of airy refinement.

Cultural Needs: Buttercup winter hazel prefers a moist, acidic, well-drained soil. It should be planted where it will not be subject to strong winds or early frost, but is otherwise undemanding.

Landscape Uses: This is an ideal edge of woods plant, used either alone or en masse. When it is in flower it appears to glow; afterward it settles contentedly but inconspicuously among the surrounding plants. Its flowers will be most prominent if viewed against an evergreen background. One of the most striking displays of buttercup winter hazel is at the garden at Winterthur in Delaware, where the sight of it blooming alongside the deep lavender flowers of *Rhododendron mucronulatum* along the famous March Walk is breathtaking.

Insects and Diseases: Buttercup winter hazel has no serious pests or diseases.

Dirca palustris

COMMON NAME:
LEATHERWOOD

Family: Thymelaeaceae
Hardiness: Zone 3–9
Shade Tolerance/Preference: Light, partial, or full shade

Habit and Mature Size: This is a densely branched shrub, oval to roundish in shape. It tends to grow 3 to 6 feet (1 to 1.8m) tall and wide, depending upon cultural conditions.

Aesthetic Value: Leatherwood is a quietly appealing plant. It has pale green leaves that are quite pretty in the autumn. The flowers appear in early spring and are a pleasing, if not dazzling, light yellow. The stems are smooth, tough, and pliable. The common name is leatherwood because the bark feels leathery and it is hard to remove a piece of broken stem. As the plant ages the older stems develop attractive fissures.

Cultural Needs: Leatherwood is native to and thrives in moist soil, preferably one rich in organic matter. It is in fact quite tolerant of wet conditions. It may be slow to recover from transplanting.

Landscape Uses: This is an interesting plant for its texture and form in a naturalistic or native plant garden. The bark of leatherwood was used by Native Americans to make baskets, bow strings, and fishing lines.

Insects and Diseases: Leatherwood has no serious pests or diseases.

Fothergilla gardenii

COMMON NAME:
DWARF FOTHERGILLA

Family: Hamamelidaceae
Hardiness: Zones 5–8
Shade Tolerance/Preference: Light shade to full sun

Habit and Mature Size: Grows 3 to 4 feet (1 to 1.2m) tall and about 3 feet (1m) wide. It is dense and has upright, spreading branches.

Aesthetic Value: Dwarf fothergilla has handsome, broadly oval leaves that are dark green in summer and absolutely golden in the fall. The flowers appear in midspring before the leaves. The flowers are white and very fragrant and are shaped like bottle brushes. Stems are pale gray, slender, and grow in an appealing zigzag pattern.

Cultural Needs: A well-drained, slightly acidic soil is ideal. In full sun in a hot climate the leaves may scorch. Water periodically if drought conditions persist.

Landscape Uses: This is an attractive and trouble-free plant that deserves wider use. It works well as a foundation plant, in a shrub border, in a mixed border, or planted in a group along the edge of a woodland garden.

Insects and Diseases: Dwarf fothergilla has no serious pests or diseases.

Cultivars: 'Blue Mist' was selected and named by the Morris Arboretum Philadelphia, Pennsylvania. It is distinguished by its powder blue foliage. 'Mt. Airy' is especially vigorous and has excellent autumn color.

Fothergilla gardenii

Hamamelis mollis

COMMON NAME:

CHINESE WITCH HAZEL

Family: Hamamelidaceae / **Hardiness:** Zones 5–8

Shade Tolerance/Preference:

Full sun or partial shade

Habit and Mature Size: This is a relatively small tree, which grows about 10 to 15 feet (3 to 4.6m) tall and 20 feet (6m) wide. It has a compact habit and an oval shape with spreading branches.

Aesthetic Value: Chinese witch hazel has perfect yellow flowers, probably the most fragrant of all the witch hazels. It begins to bloom in February and the flowers often last into March. The leaves turn a wonderful, bright yellow in the autumn.

Cultural Needs: A moist, well-drained, acidic soil rich in organic material is preferable. In periods of drought supplemental watering may be necessary, especially if the plant is grown in full sun.

Hamamelis mollis

Landscape Uses: This is an outstanding tree when planted either as a specimen or in groups. For best effect plant it with an evergreen background where it will be visible from the house. It is a good foundation plant, especially up against a stone wall. Chinese witch hazel is one of the two parents of the more common *Hamamelis* x *intermedia* (the other parent is *H. japonica*).

Insects and Diseases: Chinese witch hazel has no serious pests or diseases.

Cultivars: 'Pallida' has fragrant, sulfur yellow flowers borne in great profusion. The leaves are brighter than those of the species.

Other species: *Hamamelis virginiana* (common witch hazel) has flowers that are yellow and fragrant and appear between mid-October and December, depending upon the weather. The flowers are most effective after the leaves have dropped. The foliage color in fall is often a vibrant yellow. Zones 3–8.

Hydrangea quercifolia

COMMON NAME:

OAKLEAF HYDRANGEA

Family: Saxifragaceae

Hardiness: Zones 6–9

Shade Tolerance/Preference:

Partial shade

Habit and Mature Size: Oakleaf hydrangea grows 4 to 6 feet (1.2 to 1.8m) in a mound shape and spreads 3 to 5 feet (1 to 1.5m). In texture and form it is a coarse plant. The branches are stiff and upright and it has shallow stoloniferous roots that run along the ground and produce new plants at the tip, spreading to form a dense colony over time.

Aesthetic Value: This is a shrub that is noteworthy throughout the year. It blooms in summer and the blooms consist of large, white, sterile outer flowers and numerous small, creamy white, fertile inner flowers. Color changes gradually to pale pink and then brown; the flowers of the cultivars are definitely showier. The stems and bark of oakleaf hydrangea exfoliate in beautiful shades of cinnamon brown. The leaves are bold in shape and coarse in texture, and in autumn they are spectacular in varying shades of red, orange, and purple.

Cultural Needs: Oakleaf hydrangea requires a moist, relatively rich and well-drained soil. It can be tender as a young plant, especially in a cooler climate, and might need some added winter protection until it is well established.

Landscape Uses: The cultivars are more ornamental than the species and are useful in a shrub border or for massing under a high canopy tree.

Insects and Diseases: Leaf blight and powdery mildew may occur but are rarely serious; root fungus is sometimes a problem on older plants.

Cultivars: 'Snow Queen' has larger and more attractive flower heads.

Hydrangea quercifolia

Ilex verticillata

COMMON NAME:
WINTERBERRY
Family: Aquifoliaceae
Hardiness: Zones 3–9
Shade Tolerance/Preference:
Full sun or partial shade

Habit and Mature Size: This oval-shaped shrub has a dense habit and fine, upright stems. It is multistemmed and the bark is smooth and slate gray. As the plant matures the stems tend to arch and the overall habit becomes more fountainlike. The ultimate size of the species is 8 to 12 feet (2.4 to 3.7m) tall and equally wide.

Aesthetic Value: The main ornamental virtue of winterberry is its fruit. It has bright red berries, often in pairs, that ripen in late summer or early fall and persist into January. The sight of a grouping of winterberry in full fruit against the snow is simply spectacular.

Cultural Needs: Winterberry is native to wet, swampy woodland edges and this is the type of environment in which it will thrive. A moist soil, slightly acidic and rich in organic matter, is ideal. Both a male and a female are needed for pollination to occur and the fruit to develop.

Landscape Uses: A mass planting of winterberry is most impressive, especially if there is an evergreen background to set off the brilliant red color of the fruit. It is lovely when planted as a group alongside a stream or pond, where the fruit is reflected in the water. I have seen it grown in a container and it is truly striking against a gray winter sky. The fruit will also attract winter waterfowl and songbirds to the garden, though it is poisonous to humans.

Insects and Diseases: Winterberry has no serious pests or diseases.

Cultivars: 'Autumn Glow' has intense orange-red fruit with flashes of yellow; 'Harvest Red' has fiery red fruit and reddish purple autumn foliage; 'Scarlett O'Hara' grows 10 feet (3m) tall and about 12 feet (3.7m) wide and has a great profusion of small, clear red fruit. Not surpris-

51

ingly, the preferred pollinator is a cultivar called 'Rhett Butler'. 'Sparkleberry' also has abundant red fruit and grows about 10 to 12 feet (3 to 3.7m) tall, though a dwarf form is also available. 'Winter Red' grows about 8 feet (2.4m) tall and 10 feet (3m) wide and has a great quantity of persistent red fruit and bronze-colored autumn foliage.

Ilex verticillata

Itea virginica

COMMON NAME:
VIRGINIA SWEETSPIRE

Family: Saxifragaceae

Hardiness: Zones 6–9

Shade Tolerance/Preference: Full sun or partial shade

Habit and Mature Size: Virginia sweetspire grows 3 to 6 feet (1 to 1.8m) in height and may spread twice as wide, depending upon cultural conditions. If grown in moist soil, it will spread to form broad thickets. The stems are slender and erect and the bark is smooth when young, becoming blocky and reddish brown with age.

Aesthetic Value: The cultivar is more ornamental than the species. The species has fragrant, white upright flow-

ers in late spring and early summer. Foliage is bright green in summer and scarlet red and crimson in autumn, and will persist into early winter if the weather is mild. If grown in enough sun the young twigs and branches will be deep red in winter.

Cultural Needs: Virginia sweetspire is native to wooded streambanks and hillside bogs and is sometimes even found growing in shallow water. It thus prefers a moist garden soil, rich in organic matter. It is best to transplant this shrub balled and burlapped. Prune out the oldest stems every few years. If left alone in a conducive environment it can form large colonies over time.

Landscape Uses: Like winterberry, Virginia sweetspire can be a lovely container plant. It is also perfect for mass-

Itea virginica

ing alongside a stream or pond and is excellent for slope stabilization in a wet area.

Insects and Diseases: Virginia sweetspire has no serious pests or diseases.

Cultivars: 'Henry's Garnet' was selected for its pendulous white flowers, burgundy autumn foliage and wine red winter stems.

Kerria japonica

COMMON NAME:
JAPANESE KERRIA

Family: Rosaceae
Hardiness: Zones 5–9
Shade Tolerance/Preference: Partial, light, or full shade

Habit and Mature Size: Japanese kerria grows to an ultimate height and spread of about 6 feet (1.8m). It has graceful, slender stems and an upright, arching habit.

Aesthetic Value: In May bright yellow flowers appear and last for two to three weeks. The leaves are bright

Kerria japonica

green and narrowly tapering. The stems grow in a zigzag fashion and remain deep green through the winter.

Cultural Needs: This is a vigorous plant and will manage in less than perfect conditions. It prefers a rich, well-drained soil out of the way of winter winds. Over-fertilization will result in weedy growth. Prune after flowering in the spring and remove the oldest canes from the base every few years.

Landscape Uses: Its bright yellow flowers and elegant green stems make this a welcome addition to a shrub border or a mixed border. Japanese kerria's durabilty and sustained interest make it useful for massing in tough sites like highway borders or other public areas.

Insects and Diseases: Japanese kerria has no serious pests or diseases.

Cultivars: 'Alba' has creamy white, single flowers; 'Kin Kan' has single yellow flowers and outstanding green and yellow striped stems. 'Picta' has finer green foliage with white margins; leaves that revert to solid green should be pruned out. This cultivar grows about 4 feet (1.2m) tall. 'Pleniflora' has double, golden yellow flowers.

Rhododendron mucronulatum

COMMON NAME:
KOREAN RHODODENDRON

Family: Ericaceae
Hardiness: Zones 5–7
Shade Tolerance/Preference:
Full sun or partial shade

Habit and Mature Size: This shrub ultimately grows 4 to 6 feet (1.2 to 1.8m) high and as wide. The branches are upright and the overall form is generally oval.

Aesthetic Value: Korean rhododendron is one of the earliest shrubs to flower in the spring. The purplish rose–colored flowers are bell-shaped and appear in great profusion before the leaves emerge. The flowers are sometimes killed by late frosts. Leaves are narrowly elliptical and turn yellowish bronze in autumn.

Cultural Needs: This shrub prefers a cool, moist, well-drained and acidic soil, rich in organic matter. Mulch with pine needles or decayed oak leaf mold.

Landscape Uses: Excellent in the shrub border, Korean rhododendron is especially beautiful when combined with other early-flowering shrubs like winter hazel (*Corylopsis pauciflora*) or February daphne (*Daphne mezereum*). It is lovely under high canopy trees and planted in combination with conifers and broad-leaved evergreens.

Insects and Diseases: Wilt, rhododendron and azalea stem borers, black vine weevil, and browsing deer can all cause problems for the Korean rhododendron.

Cultivars: 'Cornell Pink' has beautiful, clear pink flowers.

Other species: *Rhododendron schlippenbachi* (royal azalea) has delicate pale to rose pink flowers that appear in April, before the leaves have emerged. The leaves are dark green in summer and turn to shades of yellow, orange, and red in autumn. Zones 4–7.

**Rhododendron mucronulatum
'Cornell Pink'**

Vaccinium corymbosum

COMMON NAME:
HIGHBUSH BLUEBERRY

Family: Ericaceae / **Hardiness:** Zones 5-7
Shade Tolerance/Preference:
Full sun (for optimum fruit production)
or light shade

Habit and Mature Size: Highbush blueberry is a multi-stemmed shrub with an upright habit and spreading branches. The overall form is irregularly rounded. Highbush blueberry puts out suckers and may form a dense thicket over time. It grows 6 to 12 feet (1.8 to 3.7m) high with an equal spread.

Aesthetic Value: In May, just as the new leaves are unfolding, small white, urn-shaped flowers appear. By summer the green fruit is ripening to a characteristic blue and finally to black. The fruit is edible and highly prized by both humans and birds. The leaves of highbush blueberry are dark green until autumn, when they turn fiery shades of yellow, bronze, orange, and red. As the weather turns colder, the twigs become bright red and are prominent in the winter landscape.

Cultural Needs: Highbush blueberry is native to acidic, marshy areas but will grow in any decent garden soil that is acidic, not too dry, and well-drained. Chlorosis (a blanching of the plant's green parts) will be a problem if the pH is not in the 4.5 to 5.5 range. Blueberries should be mulched to avoid injuries around the roots and to retain moisture. To improve fruit production prune heavily in late winter or early spring and plant more than one cultivar.

Landscape Uses: Blueberries have long been appreciated for their delicious summer fruit, but only recently has attention been paid to their value as ornamental plants. They are attractive throughout the year and work very well in a shrub or mixed border, assuming the soil is acidic. Their autumn foliage and winter twig color are exceptional. Blueberries also serve to attract birds to the garden.

Insects and Diseases: Chlorosis (caused by iron deficiency) can be a problem if the bush is planted in lime

Vaccinium corymbosum

soil or near a cement wall. Other disease and insect problems are not likely to be serious enough to warrant treatment if the plant is properly sited.

Cultivars: More than forty cultivars are commercially available. If you are interested in blueberries exclusively for their fruit, check with your local agricultural extension agent to determine the best fruiting cultivar for your area. One of the most ornamental culitvars is 'Northland'; its leaves turn bright orange in autumn.

Viburnum x juddii

COMMON NAME:

JUDD VIBURNUM

Family: Caprifoliaceae
Hardiness: Zones 4–7
Shade Tolerance/Preference: Full sun to partial shade

Habit and Mature Size: Judd viburnum grows about 6 feet (1.8m) tall and 3 to 4 feet (1 to 1.2m) wide. It has a full, rounded habit with upward-spreading branches.

Aesthetic Value: This viburnum has lovely pink to red buds that open in late April to early May. Flowers are white blusted with pink, held in clusters, and extraordinarily fragrant. The leaves are dark green and turn an attractive wine red color in fall.

Cultural Needs: Judd viburnum prefers a moist, well-drained soil rich in organic matter. A slightly acidic soil is ideal. Any pruning should be done after flowering.

Landscape Uses: Its wonderfully fragrant flowers and restrained habit make this a good plant for the foundation of a house, especially near a doorway where its flowers can best be appreciated. The flowers can be cut and brought indoors for arrangements. Judd viburnum is also splendid in a shrub border, in a mixed border, or on the edge of a woodland where it is shaded by a high canopy deciduous tree.

Insects and Diseases: This plant is more resistant to bacterial leaf spot than its parent.

Other Species: *Viburnum dilatatum* (linden viburnum) has leaves that are are dark green in summer and can be reddish to burgundy in autumn, though this is variable. The flowers appear in late May to early June. They are white, fertile, and small, and arranged in flat-topped formations known as cymes; their fragrance is musky and not terribly pleasant. The most outstanding feature of this viburnum is its fruit. Bright red berries first appear against the dark foliage in early autumn. The fruit persists through the winter and is only gradually consumed by migrating birds. The color of the fruit changes over time and by mid-December it appears purplish red. Zones 5–7.

Viburnum x juddii

EVERGREEN
SHRUBS

Skimmia japonica (male and female)

Aucuba japonica

COMMON NAME:
JAPANESE AUCUBA

Family: Cornaceae
Hardiness: Zones 7–10; may survive in Zone 6 with protection
Shade Tolerance/Preference: Full or dense shade

Habit and Mature Size: This evergreen shrub grows 5 to 10 feet (1.5 to 3m) in height and forms a dense, upright thicket. In the wild this shrub will grow vigorously.

Aesthetic Value: The leaves of Japanese aucuba are long, dark green, and glossy. The flowers are purple, and both male and female plants are needed for pollination. The fruit is an interesting scarlet, berrylike drupe (a stone fruit, like a cherry), though it is often hidden by the foliage. This plant is grown primarily for its foliage and the leaves of some of the cultivars are outstanding.

Cultural Needs: This is an extremely tough shrub and has been known to grow where other plants cannot, for instance, under mature shade trees. It prefers moist, well-drained soil rich in organic matter but will manage with less. It is tolerant of pollution and really demands only shade. If grown in sun the leaves will become sickly looking.

Landscape Uses: This is a very useful plant, particularly in a warm climate, because of its lustrous foliage and tolerance of deep shade and of less than ideal cultural conditions. It is attractive when planted in groups beneath large trees or as a foundation plant on the north or east side of a house.

Insects and Diseases: Japanese aucuba has no serious pests or diseases.

Cultivars: The cultivar 'Variegata' is the most popular form of aucuba. It is also known as the gold dust plant because it has yellow-spotted leaves. 'Mamorita' also has attractive leaves spotted with gold.

Aucuba japonica 'Marmorita'

Camellia japonica

COMMON NAMES:
JAPANESE CAMELLIA,
COMMON CAMELLIA

Family: Theaceae
Hardiness: Zones 8–9
Shade Tolerance/Preference:
Light or partial shade

Habit and Mature Size: There are several different forms of Japanese camellia recognized; most grow in a densely pyramidal shape, generally rather stiff and formal in habit. In a garden setting the species grows about 10 to 15 feet (3 to 4.6m) tall and 6 to 10 feet (1.8 to 3m) wide.

Aesthetic Value: Several hundred different cultivars of Japanese camellia are grown and there is thus a great diversity of flower colors and forms from which to choose. The flowers range in color from white to the darkest red and bloom from autumn until the following spring. The flowers of the species and of most of the cultivars are not fragrant. The leaves are dark green, very glossy, and oval in shape.

Cultural Needs: A moist, acidic, well-drained soil rich in organic matter is ideal. Plants should be mulched because of their shallow roots.

57

Camellia japonica 'Paigne'

Landscape Uses: This plant can be lovely but it is certainly overused in the southern United States. A single specimen of a choice cultivar can be charming either in a mixed or shrub border or as a foundation plant. A large grouping of camellias, however, can seem more tiresome than beautiful.

Insects and Diseases: Black mold, leaf gall, leaf spot, flower blight, stem cankers, root rot, tea scale, mealy bugs, and weevils are just a few of the problems that can plague camellias.

Cultivars: An extensive listing of the hundreds of Japanese camellia cultivars available can be obtained from the American Camellia Society in Marshall, Georgia.

Other Species: *Camellia sasanqua* (Sasanqua camellia) has leaves that are are a dark, lustrous green and are distinctly

smaller than those of the Japanese camellia. The flowers are also smaller and more open, though a great range of colors and forms is available among the cultivars of this species as well. Sasanqua camellia tends to bloom earlier than Japanese camellia, beginning in September and continuing usually well into December. The stems of *C. sasanqua*, unlike *C. japonica*, are hairy. Zones 8–9.

Cephalotaxus harringtonia *'Fastigiata'*

COMMON NAME:
FASTIGIATE JAPANESE PLUM YEW

Family: Cephalotaxaceae
Hardiness: Zones 5–9
Shade Tolerance/Preference:
Light, partial, or full shade

Habit and Mature Size: The species is not particularly ornamental and is rarely seen in gardens. This cultivar is columnar in shape when young, becoming more vase-shaped with maturity. The ultimate size is 6 feet (1.8m) tall by 5 feet (1.5m) wide.

Aesthetic Value: Fastigiate plum yew has lovely reddish-brown bark and deep green needles that are attractive throughout the year. In shape, texture, and color, this is a dense, lush, and elegant plant.

Cultural Needs: Fastigiate plum yew tolerates a wide variety of sites and withstands drought well.

Landscape Uses: This genus is in appearance very similar to the genus *Taxus* (yew). A significant difference is that white-tailed deer adore yews and seem to leave fastigiate plum yew alone. It is thus a good alternative in an environment where deer are pervasive. Use it as a low hedge or screen, as a foundation plant, or in a shrub border.

Insects and Diseases: This shrub has no serious pests or diseases.

Other Cultivars: 'Duke Gardens' is lower-growing than 'Fastigiata', maturing at about 3 feet (1m) tall and as wide or wider. 'Prostrata' stays even lower in height. Its horizontal branching habit makes it an excellent groundcover.

Fatsia japonica

COMMON NAME:

JAPANESE FATSIA

Family: Araliaceae
Hardiness: Zones 8–10
Shade Tolerance/Preference: Full shade

Habit and Mature Size: Japanese fatsia typically grows 6 to 10 feet (1.8 to 3m) tall and wide. It may grow either as a bushy shrub or as a small tree. The habit tends in any case to be more or less rounded.

Aesthetic Value: In a warm climate this is an intriguing, highly architectural plant. It has lustrous dark green leaves year-round. Leaves are huge, leathery, and deeply lobed, with individual leaves growing 10 to 14 inches

Fatsia japonica

(25.5 to 35.5cm) wide. The overall effect is very tropical. Individual flowers are small and white but are borne in large, showy, branched clusters.

Cultural Needs: Japanese fatsia can tolerate varying conditions, but prefers a slightly acidic, moist soil and will appreciate extra fertilizing. Try to protect this plant from strong winds and winter sun and ensure good air circulation.

Landscape Uses: This is a bold plant and is best used as a specimen. It creates an interesting tropical effect and should be planted in combination with plants with contrasting shapes and textures for optimum effect. Japanese fatsia would be very pleasing, for example, alongside shade-tolerant conifers or ornamental grasses.

Insects and Diseases: Spider mites may infest Japanese fatsia.

Cultivars: 'Aurea' has golden variegated leaves; 'Moseri' has larger leaves than the species but a more compact form.

Ilex glabra

COMMON NAME:

INKBERRY

Family: Aquifoliaceae
Hardiness: Zones 5–9
Shade Tolerance/Preference: Light or partial shade

Habit and Mature Size: This North American native grows about 6 feet (1.8m) tall and 8 feet (2.4m) wide. It has a roundish shape and upright, ascending branches. It tends to be dense when young but grows more open as it ages.

Aesthetic Value: Inkberry has thin, dark green leaves that are somewhat shiny on the upper side. The whitish flowers are inconspicuous, though they do attract bees.

Cultural Needs: Inkberry likes a moist, acidic soil and protection from winter winds. It is native to wet, swampy areas and is thus quite tolerant of a damp site.

Landscape Uses: This shrub is attractive used in a foundation planting, as a hedge or screen, or grouped together to form an evergreen mass. It is also useful as a background plant in a perennial border. It is best underplanted

Ilex glabra

because it may lose its lower leaves over time, depending upon the cultivar.

Insects and Diseases: Inkberry has no serious pests or diseases.

Cultivars: 'Compacta' is a dwarf, female selection with a more lush and dense habit than the species. 'Ivory Queen' has white fruit. 'Nigra' has purple leaves in the winter.

Other Species: *Ilex crenata* (Japanese holly) is one of the most shade-tolerant of all the hollies. It has small, glossy green leaves with a fine texture. The fruit is black and not particularly showy, nor are the white flowers. Zones 5–7.

Ilex × *meserveae* (Meserve holly). The Meserve hollies are, as a group, exceptionally ornamental. They have glossy leaves, a vigorous growth habit, and abundant fruit (both male and female plants are needed for pollination and fruit set). Zones 5–7.

Kalmia latifolia

COMMON NAME:
MOUNTAIN LAUREL

Family: Ericaceae
Hardiness: Zones 5–9
Shade Tolerance/Preference: Light, partial, or full shade

Habit and Mature Size: Mountain laurel grows as a large shrub, reaching 8 to 16 feet (2.4 to 5m) in height with a similar spread. In the wild it may grow up to 20 feet (6m) tall or more. It is dense when young and becomes more open and loose with age. Its overall shape is broad and mounded.

Aesthetic Value: The outstanding ornamental feature of mountain laurel is its flowers. The spaceshiplike buds seem to open magically to lighter shades of pink, rose, and white pointed and cup-shaped flowers with deep rose markings. The flowers appear in late June in clusters and have a light, pleasant fragrance. Leaves have a leathery texture and are dark green in color. The brown fruit is not particularly showy and it is poisonous to humans.

Cultural Needs: Mountain laurel prefers an acidic, well-drained soil. It prefers cool conditions and should defi-

Kalmia latifolia

nitely be grown in shade in warm climates. It has a fibrous root system and is easy to transplant. Mulch with pine needles or decayed oak leaves to retain an even soil temperature, moisture level, and pH.

Landscape Uses: This is one of the great jewels of a shady garden, used either singly or in groups. It is lovely planted along the edge of a woodland setting, in a shady corner, massed in a shrub border, or as a foundation plant along the northern or eastern side of a house. The older plants develop interesting lines and shapes and are intriguing even when not in flower.

Insects and Diseases: Azalea stem borer, rhododendron borer, leaf spot, flower blight, mulberry whitefly, scale, and lacebug may all affect mountain laurel.

Cultivars: 'Bullseye' has striking cinnamon-purple and white-colored flowers. It eventually grows 6 to 8 feet (1.8 to 2.4m) tall and 6 feet (1.8m) wide. 'Elf' is a dwarf form with pale pink buds and pure white flowers. 'Ostbo Red' has deep red buds and red flowers. 'Sarah' has red buds and pinkish red flowers. The new leaves and stems are wine red, the foliage is quite glossy, and the habit is a dense 4 to 6 feet (1.2 to 1.8m) tall.

Leucothoe fontanesiana

COMMON NAMES:

DROOPING LEUCOTHOE, FETTERBUSH

Family: Ericaceae

Hardiness: Zones 4–6

Shade Tolerance/Preference: Light, partial, or full shade

61

Habit and Mature Size: Drooping leucothoe has a graceful, spreading habit with arching branches. It slowly grows 3 to 5 feet (1 to 1.5m) tall and as wide or wider.

Aesthetic Value: This is a handsome evergreen shrub with year-round interest. The new leaves in the spring are a lustrous greenish bronze and then turn a rich, deep green. In winter the foliage has a purplish bronze cast. The flowers in May are small, white delicate racemes that are fragrant and attractively drooping.

Cultural Needs: Drooping leucothoe should be transplanted as a container plant in the spring. It prefers a moist, acidic, well-drained soil rich in organic matter. It is critical to site this plant where it will not be exposed to drying winds; otherwise the leaves become unsightly. It is not very drought-tolerant and should be well watered if dry conditions persist. Only light pruning is neces-

Leucothoe fontanesiana 'Rainbow'

sary—in spring after flowering prune out some of the oldest canes to keep mature plants open and healthy.

Landscape Uses: The fluid habit and restrained manner of drooping leucothoe make it ideal for a shady spot alongside a house or path (assuming it is not too dry), on the edge of a woodland garden, or in the front of a mixed border. It is an especially good choice as an understory plant beneath taller-growing shrubs that have a habit of losing their lower leaves.

Insects and Diseases: Leaf spot may present problems for drooping leucothoe.

Cultivars: 'Girard's Rainbow' has gorgeous new growth in varying shades of pale pink, white, orange, and bronze. 'Nana' has glossy, dark green leaves and grows 2 feet (61cm) tall by 6 feet (1.8m) wide. 'Scarletta' has extraordinarily lustrous leaves that emerge red and turn a deep green in summer. As the weather turns cold the foliage becomes an unusual purplish burgundy color and stays this way through the winter. 'Scarletta' grows only 2 feet (61cm) by 4 feet (1.2m) and makes an exciting evergreen groundcover in moist shade.

Mahonia aquifolium

COMMON NAME:
OREGON GRAPE HOLLY

Family: Berberidaceae
Hardiness: Zones 5–8
Shade Tolerance/Preference:
Light, partial, or full shade

Habit and Mature Size: Oregon grape holly becomes a narrow, coarse shrub 3 to 6 feet (1 to 1.8m) tall and 3 to 4 feet (1 to 1.2m) wide. It develops stout multiple stems with rigidly erect branches. It has a dense habit, but tends to lose the leaves on its lower stems over time.

Aesthetic Value: Oregon grape holly is more interesting than it is beautiful. It has large, compound leaves with sharp teeth along the margin. The texture is very leathery and rough. In late April through May golden yellow flowers appear in dense clusters. These are followed by waxy blue berries, probably the showiest aspect of this plant.

Mahonia aquifolium

The fruit hangs in grapelike clusters and is very appealing to birds and animals, though it is not edible by humans.

Cultural Needs: Transplant Oregon grape holly balled and burlapped into a moist, acidic, well-drained soil. In dry or overly sunny or windy conditions the leaves will scorch.

Landscape Uses: This is a bold plant and should be used with some discretion and moderation. A single specimen can be an attractive textural and structural contrast in a foundation planting or a shrub border. A small grouping is effective on the edge of a woodland, and draws birds and animals to the garden.

Insects and Diseases: Leaf spot, leaf rust, barberry aphid, scale, and whitefly may all affect Oregon grape holly.

Cultivars: 'Atropurpureum' has dark, reddish purple leaves in winter. 'Compactum' grows only about 3 feet (1m) tall and has a dense habit and very shiny leaves.

Microbiota decussata

COMMON NAME:
SIBERIAN CARPET CYPRESS

Family: Cupressaceae
Hardiness: To Zone 3
(heat tolerance not yet established)
Shade Tolerance/Preference: Sun or shade

Habit and Mature Size: This conifer has scaly needles and arching branches that create a fanlike appearance. It stays low and is flat-topped. The mature size is 2 feet (61cm) tall by 15 feet (4.6m) wide.

Aesthetic Value: The arching branches of Siberian carpet cypress are quite lacy and refined in character, giving the plant a soft overall texture. The foliage is a lush green until winter, when it turns an appealing coppery purple.

Cultural Needs: Siberian carpet cypress likes a well-drained site and is otherwise undemanding of its cultural conditions. It will withstand drought once it is established and is extremely cold-hardy. It is one of the most shade-tolerant of all conifers.

Landscape Uses: This is an excellent alternative to the ubiquitous juniper as a groundcover, especially as Siberian carpet cypress is truly tolerant of shade. It is tough and durable despite its feathery appearance. It also works well in the foreground of a shrub border or on a slope or hillside.

Insects and Diseases: Siberian carpet cypress has no serious pests or diseases.

Microbiota decussata

Osmanthus heterophyllus

COMMON NAMES:
HOLLY OSMANTHUS,
FALSE HOLLY

Family: Oleaceae
Hardiness: Zones 7–9
Shade Tolerance/Preference:
Light or partial shade

Habit and Mature Size: This is a large, very dense shrub that grows 10 to 20 feet (3 to 6m) tall and about 10 feet (3m) wide. Its form tends to be somewhat oval or rounded.

Aesthetic Value: Holly osmanthus blooms late in the season, typically in late September and October. Its whitish flowers are diminutive but exceedingly fragrant, even from a great distance. Flowers are followed by blue-black fruits in late autumn. The leaves are shiny dark green on the tops and yellowish green on the underside. Holly osmanthus gets its common name from the resemblance its leaves bear to holly plants; the leaves are pointed and very spiny, making this shrub virtually impenetrable.

Cultural Needs: Plant in fertile, moist, acidic soil in a well-drained site. At the northernmost range of its hardiness a protected site away from winter winds is recommended. Holly osmanthus will withstand a lot of pruning but this should not be necessary.

Landscape Uses: Even if it did not have its wonderfully scented flowers in autumn, holly osmanthus would still be worth growing. Its lustrous, spiny leaves make it a perfect hedge or screen. It is also lovely as a single specimen in a shrub border or alongside the foundation of a building.

Insects and Diseases: This shrub has no serious pests or diseases.

Cultivars: 'Rotundifolius' is a slow-growing dwarf form that reaches a height of 4 to 5 feet (1.2 to 1.5m).

Other Species: *Osmanthus × fortunei* is a hybrid that grows to 6 feet (1.8m); it has large, oval, spiny leaves and bears white flowers in autumn. Zones 7–9.

Pieris japonica

COMMON NAME:

JAPANESE PIERIS

Family: Ericaceae

Hardiness: Zones 5–8

Shade Tolerance/Preference: Light or partial shade or sun

Habit and Mature Size: Japanese pieris grows 8 to 12 feet (2.4 to 3.7m) tall and 6 to 8 feet (2.4m) wide. It has an upright habit and is restrained in its growth and form.

Aesthetic Value: The flowers of this species appear in early spring. They are white, urn-shaped, slightly fragrant, and hang in pendulous panicles (multistemmed flower heads) The leaves are oblong, shiny green above and pale green on the underside. When the new leaves emerge in the spring they are a glistening bronze-purple.

Cultural Needs: Japanese pieris will thrive in a moist, acidic soil rich in organic matter. It will tolerate a sandy soil better than heavy clay. It should be sheltered from winter winds and harsh summer sun, but is otherwise not fussy. Any pruning should be done after flowering in the spring. Mulching with pine needles or decayed oak leaves is advisable.

Landscape Uses: There are more and more new cultivars of Japanese pieris with a large diversity of flower and foliage colors, sizes, and forms available. If well-sited, this is an excellent choice for a foundation plant, in a shrub border, or massed under the light shade of a high canopy tree.

Insects and Diseases: Leaf spot, dieback, lacebug (especially pernicious in the eastern United States), Florida wax scale, nematodes, and two-spotted mites may all pester Japanese pieris.

Cultivars: 'Dorothy Wycoff' has dark red flower buds that open to deep pink flowers; its form is compact. 'Flamingo' has rich, rosy red flowers and very glossy new growth. 'Mountain Fire' has fiery red new leaves and white flowers. 'Variegata' has white flowers and green leaves with white margins. Grow this cultivar in shade for best effect.

Prunus laurocerasus

COMMON NAMES:

CHERRY LAUREL, ENGLISH LAUREL

Family: Rosaceae

Hardiness: Zones 6–7

Shade Tolerance/Preference:

Light, partial, or full shade or sun

Habit and Mature Size: In the wild old specimens have been known to reach 20 to 25 feet (6 to 7.5m) in height. In cultivation a range of 10 to 15 feet (3 to 4.6m) tall and 15 feet (4.6m) wide is more likely, and most of the cultivars available stay even smaller. The habit is wide-spreading and very dense.

Aesthetic Value: Perfect white flowers appear in May; they are cloyingly fragrant. The leaves are oblong in shape and lustrous green on the upper side.

Cultural Needs: A moist, well-drained soil rich in organic matter is ideal. Cherry laurel is tolerant of salt spray but does not like to be overfertilized. Root decline may occur if drainage and air circulation are poor.

65

Pieris japonica

Prunus laurocerasus

Landscape Uses: Cherry laurel makes an excellent hedge, particularly in relatively warm climates. The cultivars, of which there are more than forty, are more ornamental than the species.

Insects and Diseases: Cherry laurel is not as prone to insects and disease as other members of the cherry family; leaf shot-hole, a bacterial disease, can be disfiguring.

Cultivars: 'Forest Green' has broad, dark green foliage. It is cold-hardier than the species and grows 4 to 6 feet (1.2 to 1.8m) tall. 'Latifolia' has the largest leaves of any cultivar (12 inches, 30.5cm). The leaves are shiny and deep green. This is tall growing and can be trained into a tree. 'Otto Luyken' has a dense, compact form and tolerates very deep shade. 'Schipkaensis' has narrow, dark green leaves and grows much wider than tall. It is hardy to Zone 5.

Rhododendron carolinianum

COMMON NAME:

CAROLINA RHODODENDRON

Family: Ericaceae

Hardiness: Zone 5–8

Shade Tolerance/Preference:

Light, partial, or full shade or sun

Habit and Mature Size: This shrub grows in a mound shape 4 to 6 feet (1.2 to 1.8m) tall and equally wide. The stems are upright and the branches are irregularly ascending. Carolina rhododendron has a more refined form and texture than some other rhododendrons, such as Catawba rhododendron.

Aesthetic Value: This North American native has white to rose pink funnel-shaped flowers that bloom in May. The evergreen leaves are 2 to 3 inches (5 to 7.5cm) long and dark green; in cool climates they take on a purplish cast.

Cultural Needs: Like all rhododendrons, Carolina rhododendron requires acidic, well-drained soil rich in organic matter. The roots are shallow and should thus be mulched with pine needles or decayed oak leaves. Protec-

Rhododendron carolinianum

tion from drying winter sun, wind, and salt is very important. Pruning may not be necessary, but if done it should be soon after flowering.

Landscape Uses: This species is attractive planted in groups in a shrub border or woodland edge. It makes a fine screen or hedge, and a single specimen integrated into a foundation planting can be very effective.

Insects and Diseases: Rhododendrons are prone to many insects and diseases. Proper siting will help minimize problems. Dieback, leaf spots, gray blight, crown rot, shoot blight, nematodes, thrips, scales, and rhododendron tip midge are among the potential pests and diseases.

Varieties: The variety *album* has white flowers and is later blooming than the species. The variety *luteum* has yellow flowers.

Other Species: *Rhododendron catawbiense* (Catawba rhododendron) has flowers that are lilac to rose-purple and borne in large trusses in spring. The leaves are 3 to 6 inches (7.5 to 15cm) long, leathery in texture, and dark green in color. Zones 4–8.

Rhododendron 'Gable Hybrids' (Gable Hybrid azaleas) come in a great diversity of flower colors and sizes. They bloom in late April to early May and most have small, shiny, dark green leaves.

Rhododendron catawbiense

Rhododendron '*James Gable*'

Sarcococca hookerana *var.* humilis

COMMON NAME:
SWEET BOX

Family: Buxaceae
Hardiness: Zones 6–9
Shade Tolerance/Preference: Partial to full shade

Habit and Mature Size: This is a low-growing, stoloniferous shrub. It is only 2 feet (61cm) tall at maturity and is wide-spreading via suckers.

Aesthetic Value: Sweet box has attractively shiny, dark green leaves. In spring it bears small, whitish, fragrant flowers. Male and female flowers are separate on the same plant. The small berrylike fruit is black or dark red in color.

Cultural Needs: Sweet box likes an acidic, well-drained, fertile soil. Protection from winter sun and wind will keep the foliage from drying and yellowing. Any pruning of old stems should be done in early spring to allow the more vigorous young stems to develop from the rootstock.

Landscape Uses: This variety is hardier than the straight species and makes an unusual and persistently attractive groundcover in the shade.

Insects and Diseases: Sweet box has no serious pests or diseases.

Sarcococca hookerana *var.* humilis

Skimmia japonica

COMMON NAME:
JAPANESE SKIMMIA

Family: Rutaceae
Hardiness: Zones 7–9
Shade Tolerance/Preference: Light, partial, or full shade

Habit and Mature Size: Japanese skimmia grows slowly to 3 to 5 feet (1 to 1.5m) tall and wide. Its habit is dense and dome-shaped.

Aesthetic Value: The primary attractions of this plant are its whorled, bright green leaves and the lively red fruit on the female plants. A male is needed for pollination and fruit production (one male to six females should ensure good fruit set). The fruit usually persists until spring. The flowers of Japanese skimmia are reddish in bud and open to creamy-white panicles which are slightly fragrant; the flowers on male plants are larger.

Cultural Needs: Best to transplant container-grown plants into moist, acidic soil enriched with organic matter. Little or no pruning is necessary. In the northern range of hardiness, some protection from winter wind and sun is advisable. *Skimmia reevesiana*, a related species, is slightly more cold-hardy than *S. japonica*.

Landscape Uses: This is a plant with superior form, texture, foliage color, and vibrant fruit. It works well in a foundation planting, shrub border, or mixed border. It is also attractive on a shady slope, and the lower-growing *Skimmia reevesiana* makes a good shady groundcover.

Insects and Diseases: Japanese skimmia has no serious pests or diseases.

Skimmia japonica 'Nymans'

Taxus baccata *'Repandens'*

COMMON NAMES:
SPREADING ENGLISH YEW,
COMMON YEW

Family: Taxaceae
Hardiness: Zones 6–8
Shade Tolerance/Preference:
Sun or light, partial, or full shade

Habit and Mature Size: This form of English yew will eventually grow 4 to 6 feet (1.2 to 1.8m) tall and 10 feet (3m) wide. The tips of the branches are pendulous, giving the plant a graceful, slightly arching appearance.

Aesthetic Value: This and other English yews have shiny, slightly curved needles. The needles are dark green above and dull green on the underside. Fruit is olive brown in color.

Cultural Needs: Yews prefer a well-drained soil with a neutral pH. Good drainage is probably the most critical cultural consideration. They also prefer a site away from harsh winds—drying winter winds cause the needles to turn yellow or brown—and in neither extreme heat nor extreme cold. Yews tolerate pruning well, but careful selection of the species and cultivar most appropriate for your site should minimize the need for much pruning. Any pruning should not be done late in the season.

Landscape Uses: This is an excellent plant to cover a slope, as a groundcover under trees, as a foundation plant, or in a shrub border. In areas with a large white-tailed deer population, yews are likely to be heavily browsed and an alternative is Japanese plum yew.

69

Insects and Diseases: Yew-gall midge, Taxus mealybug, black vine weevil, and Taxus scale are all potential problems.

Other Cultivars: 'Aurea' is taller growing and has golden-colored new growth. 'Fastigiata' is rigidly upright, the upper needles are almost blackish green, and the ultimate height may be 40 feet (12m) or more.

Other Species: *Taxus cuspidata* 'Nana' (Dwarf Japanese yew) has thick, dense foliage and colorful, abundant red fruit. Zones 4–7.

PERENNIALS

Aconitum carmichaelii

Aconitum carmichaelii (A. fischeri)

COMMON NAME:
AZURE MONKSHOOD

Family: Ranunculaceae
Hardiness: Zones 3–7
Shade Tolerance/Preference:
Full sun or light, partial, or full shade

Habit and Mature Size: Monkshood grows 3 to 4 feet (1 to 1.2m) tall and has a stiff, erect habit.

Aesthetic Value: In late summer deep blue flowers appear arranged in stiff panicles. The individual flowers are hooded and look like Roman helmets. They make a fine cut flower. The leaves are large, thick, and dark green. They are deeply divided and attractive from spring until frost.

Cultural Needs: Monkshood likes a rich, moist, well-drained soil. It has thick fleshy roots that do not like to be disturbed, so plant it where it is not likely to have to be moved. The roots are poisonous. They are also rather brittle and easily damaged. Space plants 2 to 3 feet (61cm to 1m) apart and plant the crowns just below the soil surface. Staking may be necessary.

Landscape Uses: Monkshoods are wonderful for their late, soft blue flowers and bold foliage. If grown in shade they are best combined with lighter-colored flowering plants to intensify the blue of the monkshoods. They are lovely, for example, planted alongside white Japanese anemones or white or pink turtlehead.

Insects and Diseases: Cyclamen mites are a potential pest.

Cultivars: 'Arendsii' is a superb cultivar that bears deep purple-blue flowers on 3- to 4-foot (1- to 1.2-cm) stems.

Other Species: *Aconitum orientale* (creamy monkshood) has lovely, creamy yellow flowers on stems that may grow 4 to 6 feet (1.2 to 1.8 cm) tall. While this species is not as upright as its shorter cousin, *A. carmichaelii*, it can make an enchanting picture in the late summer or autumn garden. Stake the flowers or plant them where they can bow over without disturbing nearby plants.

Ajuga reptans

COMMON NAME:
COMMON BUGLEWEED

Family: Labiatae
Hardiness: Zones 3–9
Shade Tolerance/Preference:
Bugleweed will tolerate sun or shade, but in warm climates it is best planted in shade

Habit and Mature Size: Bugleweed is a low, spreading groundcover. The species grows only 4 to 10 inches (10 to 25.5cm) tall and the size among the cultivars is variable. *Ajuga* creeps rapidly via underground stems and tends to form dense colonies.

Aesthetic Value: The leaves of common bugleweed are dark green or bronze and roughly oval-shaped. In a mild winter the leaves will be evergreen. The flowers are a handsome bluish purple and appear in spring in rigid, vertical spikes. The foliage and flowers of some of the cultivars are truly extraordinary.

Cultural Needs: Bugleweed is exceptionally tough and will even tolerate dry, infertile shade. Ideal conditions

Ajuga reptans

are moist soil enriched with organic matter. Keep in mind that this is a plant that tends to run aggressively and either restrain it or plant it where its invasive nature is not a problem. Good drainage and air circulation will minimize problems.

Landscape Uses: This is one of the best groundcovers available for sun or shade. It is persistently attractive and remarkably resistant to heat and drought. The cultivars are more ornamental than the species.

Insects and Diseases: Aphids, mildew, and crown rot may all affect bugleweed. Crown rot will cause whole sections to die out but can be prevented by cleaning up fallen leaves in autumn and maintaining good air circulation.

Cultivars: 'Bronze Beauty' has burgundy-bronze leaves that become more intensely colored as the weather cools. 'Burgundy Glow' has multicolored leaves in shades of pink, white, and green against electric blue flowers. 'Jungle Beauty' has tall, blue flower spikes and bold, leathery mahogony-purple leaves. 'Silver Beauty' has green and white variegated foliage and 6-inch (15cm) tall, blue flower spikes.

Alchemilla mollis

COMMON NAME:
LADY'S–MANTLE

Family: Rosaceae
Hardiness: Zones 3–8
Shade Tolerance/Preference:
Light or partial shade
(or sun in cool climates)

Habit and Mature Size: Forms a neat clump 10 to 12 inches (25.5 to 30.5cm) tall.

Aesthetic Value: The soft, fuzzy leaves of lady's-mantle are attractive from early spring until very late autumn. The leaves are large, light green, and slightly cupped. They are a lovely sight early in the morning when they hold small drops of dew. Numerous clusters of chartreuse flowers rise on wiry stems in the late spring and early summer. The flowers are long-lasting and good for fresh or dried arrangements.

Cultural Needs: *Alchemilla* likes a rich, moist soil. If grown in too much sun or overly dry conditions, the leaves become tattered and unsightly and need to be cut back. Overgrown clumps can be divided in spring or autumn.

Landscape Uses: Plant lady's-mantle where you will notice how beautiful the leaves look with the summer dew still upon them. Place it in small groups along a path or in the front of a perennial border. It is charming combined with blue-leaved hostas, rue, or astilbes.

Insects and Diseases: Lady's-mantle has no serious pests or diseases.

Amsonia hubrectii

COMMON NAME:
ARKANSAS AMSONIA

Family: Apocynaceae
Hardiness: Zones 6–8
Shade Tolerance: Full sun or light or partial shade

Habit and Mature Size: This clump-forming native plant grows about 3 feet (1m) tall and 2 to 3 feet (61cm to 1m) wide. It has a much finer texture and form than the better-known *A. tabernaemontana*.

Aesthetic Value: In spring, tiny, grayish blue star-shaped flowers appear at the tips of the leaves. The flowers are interesting but not terribly ornamental. The great charm of this plant is its foliage, which is delicate, needlelike, and gracefully whorled. These leaves give the plant the appearance of a soft and refined young pine tree. The leaves are clear green in the spring and summer; relatively late in autumn they become a breathtaking golden yellow.

Cultural Needs: Arkansas amsonia prefers a well-drained soil but is otherwise undemanding. It is very tolerant of drought and heat, especially once it is well established. Transplanting should be in spring or autumn and once planted it does not especially like to be moved. Keep the plants bushy by cutting them back by one-third after flowering.

Landscape Uses: This is a plant that deserves to be more widely known. It is beautiful and carefree if allowed to naturalize along the edge of a stream or woodland. The

Amsonia hubrectii

color and texture of its foliage also work well in a mixed border. It is striking if planted in groups alongside ornamental grasses or other herbaceous perennials with markedly contrasting foliage.

Insects and Diseases: Arkansas amsonia has no serious pests or diseases.

Anemone x hybrida

COMMON NAME:

JAPANESE ANEMONE

Family: Ranunculaceae / **Hardiness:** Zones 5–8

Shade Tolerance/Preference:

Sun or light or partial shade (afternoon shade)

Habit and Mature Size: Japanese anemones grow 3 to 5 feet (1 to 1.5m) tall. They have a mound of foliage at the base and numerous upright flowering stems above.

Aesthetic Value: The flowers appear on the wiry stems toward the end of summer. The colors will vary by cultivar but tend to be in the white to pink range; some cultivars have single and some have double flowers.

Cultural Needs: Japanese anemones prefer a moist, fertile soil and may need supplemental watering in the event of a drought. A well-drained soil is important, otherwise the plants may succumb to wet winter conditions. Individual plants should be lifted and divided every few years.

Landscape Uses: These are excellent in a perennial or mixed border because of their attractive foliage and dainty, late-blooming flowers in soft colors. They are also lovely planted en masse along the edge of a woodland as long as the shade is not too dense. They combine well with lobelias or asters; you might also plant them in front of spring-blooming bulbs, for the foliage of the Japanese anemones will mask the dying bulb foliage.

Anemone x hybrida 'Max Vogel'

Insects and Diseases: Japanese anemones have no serious pests or diseases.

Cultivars: 'Alba' grows 3 feet (1m) tall and has single white flowers. 'Honorine Jobert' has 4-foot (1.2m) stems and glorious white flowers. 'Margarete' has deep pink, semidouble flowers atop 3-foot (1m) stems. 'Pamina' is a relatively new introduction, growing only 30 inches (76cm) tall with double, lilac-colored flowers. 'Max Vogel' has semidouble, rosy pink flowers.

Aquilegia canadensis

COMMON NAME:
WILD COLUMBINE

Family: Ranunculaceae
Hardiness: Zones 4–8
Shade Tolerance/Preference:
Light or partial shade

Habit and Mature Size: This delightful eastern wildflower grows 1 to 2 feet (30.5 to 61cm) tall.

Aesthetic Value: For several weeks in spring, wild columbine is flush with red and yellow flowers. The foliage is bluish green and gracefully divided and lobed.

Cultural Needs: Columbines like a light, moist soil that is well-drained. They are by nature short-lived and tend not to last more than three or four years. They do self-sow and interbreed in the garden, so while the species or cultivar you plant may not return after a few years, you will discover that new forms have evolved. This is fine up to a point, but it is best not to plant native and exotic species together because the exotic ones will eventually dominate and you will end up with duller, less-impressive flowers.

Landscape Uses: Because of its diminutive size and freely flowering habit, this is an ideal plant for a rock garden or the front of a perennial border, or planted en masse on the edge of a woodland. Wild columbine can tolerate dry shade and is thus well-suited for a rock wall as well.

Insects and Diseases: Leaf miners make tracks through the leaves but are not fatal to the plant.

Cultivars: 'Corbett' has pale yellow flowers.

Arisaema triphyllum

COMMON NAME:
JACK-IN-THE-PULPIT

Family: Araceae / **Hardiness:** Zones 4–9
Shade Tolerance/Preference: Light, partial, or full shade

Habit and Mature Size: 1 to 3 feet (30.5cm to 1m) tall.

Aesthetic Value: This is a classic eastern woodland plant. Each plant has two leaves, each divided into 3- to

Arisaema triphyllum

take several years to reach flowering size. This is a woodland native and should be protected from heat, drought, and afternoon sun. Jack-in-the-pulpit is not poisonous, but all parts of the plant contain a bitter element that is very irritating to the mouth and throat if swallowed.

Landscape Uses: This is a good plant to naturalize on the edge of a woodland, especially under deciduous shade. It is lovely in a shady wildflower garden planted alongside native columbines, bleeding-hearts, and ferns.

Insects and Diseases: Slugs are potential pests.

Aruncus dioicus

COMMON NAME:
GOATSBEARD

Family: Rosaceae
Hardiness: Zones 4–8
Shade Tolerance/Preference:
Light or partial shade

Habit and Mature Size: Goatsbeard has an open, mounded shape and grows 4 to 6 feet (1.2 to 1.8m) tall and up to 4 feet (1.2m) wide.

Aesthetic Value: The foliage of goatsbeard is both bold and feathery. The leaves are dark green, pinnately compound, and attractive throughout the growing season. In early summer, creamy white flower plumes are held above the foliage on stout stems. The flowers are remi-

Aquilegia canadensis

6-inch (7.5 to 15cm) long segments. The leaves frame the green- and purple-striped hoodlike spathe, which arches gracefully over the shorter, greenish yellow to white spadex. These unusual and structurally complex flowers appear in spring and are followed by a brilliant cluster of red fruit in the autumn.

Cultural Needs: Jack-in-the-pulpit likes a moist soil rich in organic matter. This species of *Arisaema* will actually tolerate poorly drained soil. Plants grown from seed

niscent of astilbes. Goatsbeard is dioecious, that is, male and female flowers are on separate plants.

Cultural Needs: Goatsbeard will thrive in ordinary soil as long as there is adequate moisture. Mulch the plants to keep them from drying out.

Landscape Uses: The strong form and foliage of *Aruncus dioicus* makes it a fine specimen plant in a mixed or

Aruncus dioicus

shrub border—just be sure to leave enough room for it to grow well. It is also excellent when planted in groups alongside a stream or pond or on the edge of a woodland. A smaller but related species, *A. aethusifolius*, grows only 12 to 15 inches (30.5 to 38cm) tall and has outstanding autumn foliage.

Insects and Diseases: Goatsbeard has no serious pests or diseases.

Cultivars: 'Kneiffii' matures at 3 feet (1m) and has finely cut foliage.

Asarum europaeum

COMMON NAME:
EUROPEAN WILD GINGER

Family: Aristolochiaceae
Hardiness: Zones 4–8
Shade Tolerance/Preference:
Light, partial, or full shade

Habit and Mature Size: European wild ginger has a slowly spreading habit and creeps via horizontal stems that lay just below the ground. A mature plant grows only 6 to 8 inches (15 to 20.5cm) tall and will eventually form a sizable patch.

Aesthetic Value: The glossy, heart-shaped leaves of European wild ginger are its main attribute. The leaves are evergreen, though the old leaves may need to be cleared away in the spring to keep the plant looking tidy. The flowers are inconspicuous (they are pollinated by gnats).

Cultural Needs: This and other wild gingers like a moist, humus-rich, slightly acidic soil. They are easily increased by division in the spring or autumn. New clumps should be planted no more than 1 inch (2.5cm) deep.

Landscape Uses: European wild ginger makes an elegant groundcover because of its lustrous leaves. It is superb in a shady rock garden and offers pleasing foliage contrast when planted with ferns, narrow-leaved hostas, or crested iris. It also has a pleasing carpet effect when massed beneath trees, where other plants often falter because of root competition.

Insects and Diseases: Slugs and snails may pose problems.

Asarum europaeum

Astilbe x arendsii

COMMON NAME:

HYBRID ASTILBE

Family: Saxifragaceae

Hardiness: Zones 3–9

Shade Tolerance/Preference: Partial, light, or full shade

Habit and Mature Size: Most of these hybrids form an airy mound of foliage 12 to 18 inches (30.5 to 46cm) high. The stiff flower stems are held 12 to 18 inches (30.5 to 46cm) above the foliage.

Aesthetic Value: Astilbes are engaging throughout the growing season. The foliage is finely dissected and bright to dark green, though some cultivars have bronze-green leaves. Even when not in bloom, these are exceedingly handsome plants. The abundant flowers bloom in early summer and are held above the foliage on dark stems. The flower color, shape, and bloom time will vary by cultivar.

Cultural Needs: Astilbes prefer a slightly acidic soil rich in organic matter. They require that the soil is consistently moist but not soggy—in dry conditions the leaves will brown, but in an overly wet site the plants will rot. Mulching is advisable; apply a slow-release fertilizer each spring, and dig up and divide the plants every three to four years in spring or autumn to ensure optimum flowering. The seed heads can be left on after flowering for winter interest.

77

Landscape Uses: If you select carefully, you can have astilbes blooming in your garden from June into August. Their fernlike foliage enlivens the garden and their feathery flowers are a captivating sight grouped in a perennial border, alongside the edge of a stream or pond, or along a shady path. Combine them with bold-leaved hostas or coralbells for a persistently interesting composition.

Insects and Diseases: Astilbes have no serious pests or diseases.

Cultivars: 'Bressingham Beauty' has deep pink flowers in late July. 'Bridal Veil' grows only 2 feet (61cm) tall and has clean white flowers in July. 'Deutschland' is one of the best white-flowering astilbes and blooms early. 'Fanal' has cherry red flowers and bronzy red foliage. 'Peach Blossom' has exquisite apricot flowers in July. 'Rheinland' bears deep rose flowers in late June.

Other Species: *Astilbe chinensis* 'Pumila' (dwarf Chinese astilbe) has dark green, sharply incised compound leaves. In July and August a great profusion of stiff, chalky pink flower panicles are held rigidly above the foliage. Zones 4–8.

Begonia grandis

COMMON NAME:

HARDY BEGONIA

Family: Begoniaceae / **Hardiness:** Zones 6–8
Shade Tolerance/Preference: Partial or full shade

Habit and Mature Size: This is an upright and open plant growing 2 to 3 feet (61cm to 1m) tall.

Aesthetic Value: Hardy begonia has large, almost tropical leaves and succulent stems. The leaves are bright green above and pale green on the underside with interesting red veins and hairs. The flowers appear in September and October. They are pale pink and held in loose, drooping flat-topped flower heads. After flowering, pink seedpods are held in the axils of the upper leaves.

Cultural Needs: Hardy begonias like an evenly moist soil rich in organic matter. They leaf out late in the spring, so it is a good idea to mark where in the garden they have been planted.

Astilbe x arendsii

Begonia grandis

Landscape Uses: A grouping of hardy begonias is very effective in a shady perennial border or along a woodland path. They combine well with hostas, Siberian irises, Japanese anemones, or wild ginger.

Insects and Diseases: Hardy begonia has no serious pests or diseases.

Cultivars: 'Alba' has pure white flowers.

Bergenia cordifolia

COMMON NAME:

HEARTLEAF BERGENIA

Family: Saxifragaceae / **Hardiness:** Zones 3–9
Shade Tolerance/Preference: Light or partial shade

Habit and Mature Size: Heartleaf bergenia forms a 12-inch (30.5cm) tall dense clump.

Aesthetic Value: The foliage of heartleaf bergenia is large and leathery with a shiny luster. The leaves are bright green in spring and summer and turn a rich

Bergenia cordifolia

mahogony-bronze as the weather turns colder. In spring deep pink flower clusters appear just above the foliage.

Cultural Needs: Bergenias like a moist soil but are otherwise undemanding. They perform better in a relatively cool climate and in soil that is not overly fertilized. Clumps should be dug up and divided every few years, and the old foliage should be cleaned up in the spring before the new leaves emerge.

Landscape Uses: This is a plant that is best used, singly or in groups, where its cabbagelike foliage can be observed at close range. It can be splendid along a path or in the front of a mixed border, and its leaves are highly prized in arrangements.

Insects and Diseases: Slugs may present a problem.

Cultivars: 'Perfecta' has purplish leaves and deep rose-colored flowers. 'Purpurea' has leaves that are larger and redder than the species, and which become purple in winter. The flowers are reddish purple on colorful red stalks.

Chelone lyonii

COMMON NAME:

PINK TURTLEHEAD

Family: Scrophulariaceae
Hardiness: Zones 4–8
Shade Tolerance/Preference:
Sun or light or partial shade

Habit and Mature Size: Dense and upright to 3 feet (1m).

Aesthetic Value: Pink turtlehead has coarse, dark green leaves and bright pink hooded flowers that stand out in the shade. The flowers appear in late summer. The common name arose because the flowers look like the head of a turtle with its mouth open. The seed heads that follow are also ornamental.

Cultural Needs: Turtleheads are native to wet areas and they require an evenly moist soil. Good air circulation will also ensure healthy plants. Pinch them back in late spring, as you would asters and chrysanthemums, to keep them from becoming leggy.

Chelone lyonii

Chrysogonum virginianum

Landscape Uses: Turtleheads brighten the garden in late summer with their cheerful flowers and handsome green leaves. They will thrive along a stream or pond where they are sure to receive the moisture they need. Combine them with other late-blooming, moisture-loving perennials like monkshood and blue lobelia.

Insects and Diseases: Turtlehead has no serious pests or diseases.

Chrysogonum virginianum

COMMON NAMES:

GREEN-AND-GOLD, GOLDENSTAR

Family: Compositae

Hardiness: To Zone 5

Shade Tolerance/Preference:

Light or partial shade

Habit and Mature Size: Green-and-gold grows only 6 to 10 inches (15 to 25.5cm) tall and makes a fine ground cover.

Aesthetic Value: The small, hairy, forest green leaves of green-and-gold are covered in bright yellow, daisylike flowers on and off from spring until summer. Flowering will be more prolonged in cooler climates. In warm climates the leaves may be evergreen.

Cultural Needs: Green-and-gold likes a well-drained, moderately fertile soil that is neither too wet nor too dry.

Landscape Uses: Plant this long-blooming native along a woodland path, in a rock garden, or in the shade of a deciduous tree as a groundcover. It is tough and carefree, and its golden flowers are a great delight.

Insects and Diseases: Green-and-gold has no serious pests or diseases.

Cimicifuga racemosa

COMMON NAMES:

BUGBANE,
BLACK SNAKEROOT

Family: Ranunculaceae

Hardiness: Zones 3–8

Shade Tolerance/ Preference:

Light or partial shade

Habit and Mature Size: Bugbane forms a lush mound of foliage 2 to 3 feet (61cm to 1m) tall and about 2 feet (61cm) wide. In bloom the ultimate height of the plant is 5 to 7 feet (1.5 to 2m), though it does not give a dense or heavy appearance because the flowers are carried on slender stems.

Cimicifuga racemosa

Aesthetic Value: In late summer wandlike racemes of creamy white flowers rise up above the foliage in a stunning display. The flowers are fragrant though some find the odor offensive (insects dislike it, which is how the common name arose). The flowers last for weeks and are followed by interesting black seedpods. Foliage is bronze when it first emerges in spring and then becomes very dark green. The texture is feathery.

Cultural Needs: Bugbane prefers a well-drained soil rich in organic matter. The most critical cultural consideration is water—it must have adequate moisture or the leaf margins will brown.

Landscape Uses: This is a plant that has both a graceful texture and a bold structure. It is a good choice for naturalizing along the edge of a woodland if there is adequate space and light. It is also effective in a shrub border or toward the back of a perennial border. It is very appealing planted alongside a large-leaved hosta like *H. sieboldiana* or with some of the native shade-tolerant lilies.

Insects and Diseases: Leaf spots and rust are potential problems.

Convallaria majalis

COMMON NAME:
LILY OF THE VALLEY

Family: Liliacea
Hardiness: Zones 3–8
Shade Tolerance/Preference:
Light, partial, or full shade

81

Habit and Mature Size: Lily of the valley grows 6 to 12 inches (15 to 30.5cm) tall and its habit is upright and erect.

Aesthetic Value: The great appeal of this plant are the nodding, fragrant racemes of bell-shaped flowers that appear above the medium green leaves in midspring. Later on, bright red berries appear, though usually not in great quantities.

Cultural Needs: Lilies of the valley are among the toughest of plants and will survive in adverse soil condi-

Convallaria majalis

tions. Ideally, they should be planted in well-drained soil rich in organic matter. The fleshy rhizomes, known as pips, should be planted about 1 inch (2.5cm) deep in early spring or autumn, and a top dressing of compost once a year is advisable. The leaves tend to look a bit tattered by late summer and there is not much that can be done about this. Plantings should be thinned when flowering becomes sparse.

Landscape Uses: This makes a fine groundcover, especially under low-growing deciduous trees or conifers. It will manage where other herbaceous plants would not. The rootstocks and berries are poisonous.

Insects and Diseases: Stem rot, anthracnose, and leaf spots are all potential problems.

Cultivars: 'Rosea' has pink flowers. 'Striata' has green leaves with thin white stripes.

Corydalis lutea

COMMON NAME:
CORYDALIS

Family: Fumariaceae
Hardiness: Zones 5–10
Shade Tolerance/Preference:
Light or partial shade

Habit and Mature Size: Corydalis grows as a lacy mound 8 to 12 inches (20.5 to 30.5cm) tall.

Aesthetic Value: This is one of the longest-blooming perennials, flowering on and off from March until frost. Flowering slows down when the weather is hot. The flowers are bright yellow, tubular in shape, and look like tiny snapdragons. They are held above the leaves on long stalks. The foliage is bluish green and has a fernlike, delicate texture.

Cultural Needs: Corydalis prefers a light, sharply drained soil slightly on the acidic side. It may self-sow here and there in the garden, but not in an offensive manner. New seedlings are easily lifted.

Landscape Uses: This is a perfect plant for a rock wall, along the edge of a path, or the front of a perennial bor-

Corydalis lutea

der. Although the seed is hard to germinate, it will happily sow itself in and thrive in the most inhospitable sites, among the paving stones of a walkway for instance. Another species of corydalis worth growing is *C. cheilanthifolia*. It has exquisite ferny foliage and, though short-lived, is spectacular in a shady rock wall.

Insects and Diseases: Corydalis has no serious pests or diseases.

Dicentra spectabilis

COMMON NAME:
BLEEDING-HEART

Family: Fumariaceae
Hardiness: Zones 3–8
Shade Tolerance/Preference:
Light or partial shade

Habit and Mature Size: This old-fashioned favorite grows about 3 feet (1m) tall and has an open, slightly arching habit.

Aesthetic Value: Beginning in late April, heart-shaped flowers hang charmingly on tall, drooping stems. The outer petals of the flowers are rose red with the tips turned back and the white inner petals poking through

Dicentra spectabilis

Dicentra eximia

the outer petals. Flowering persists for several weeks. The foliage is deep green and dissected, though not as finely as other species of dicentra.

Cultural Needs: Bleeding-heart prefers a moist, rich, well-drained soil. Once it is planted, it is best not to move it. The foliage goes dormant by midsummer and should be removed once it turns yellow and pulls easily out of the ground (i.e., treat it like bulb foliage).

Landscape Uses: Bleeding-heart is perfect for early bloom in a cottage garden or perennial border, but be sure to site it where the dying foliage will not be visible. It is also effective in containers or on the edge of a woodland garden.

Insects and Diseases: Stem rot, storage rot, and wilt may occur if drainage is poor.

Cultivars: 'Alba' has pure white flowers but is not as vigorous as the species.

Other Species: *Dicentra eximia* (Wild bleeding-heart, fringed bleeding-heart) is one of the longest-blooming perennials for the shade. Flowering begins in April and is heaviest throughout the spring. As temperatures rise in

the summer flowering continues but not as intensely; it picks up again in the cooler days of autumn until frost. The flowers are pale to deep pink in color and narrowly heart-shaped. They nod in loose panicles on slender stalks known as scapes. The foliage is grayish green, finely dissected, and consistently attractive. Zones 4–8.

Digitalis purpurea

COMMON NAME:
COMMON FOXGLOVE

Family: Scrophulariaceae
Hardiness: Zones 4–8
Shade Tolerance/Preference:
Full sun or partial shade

Habit and Mature Size: Common foxglove grows 2 to 4 feet (61cm to 1.2m) tall and has an erect habit. While it is technically a biennial, it reliably self-sows and thus remains year after year in the garden.

Aesthetic Value: In late May and June great spikes of large tubular flowers rise above the foliage. The flowers are mainly purple but sometimes pink, white, or yellow,

Digitalis purpurea

and the inside is generally spotted. The leaves are huge and covered in a soft down. They are pale green in color and form dense rosettes.

Cultural Needs: Foxgloves like a moist, humus-rich soil. They should be watered during dry spells. Cut the flower stalks back to the ground after blooming unless you want the plant to self-sow (in that event leave at least one flower stalk with seeds). The seeds can also be directly sown in late summer; flowering usually occurs the second year.

Landscape Uses: This is a classic cottage garden plant and is glorious when in bloom. The long, colorful flower spikes draw your eye upward and provide an essential vertical accent in the garden. Foxgloves are wonderful combined with hostas, ferns, and bellflowers.

Insects and Diseases: Powdery mildew, leaf spot, and root and stem rots are potential problems.

Cultivars: 'Alba' has white flowers. 'Excelsior' has dense flower spikes in a wide range of colors. 'Foxy' grows only about 2 feet (61cm) tall and blooms the first year from seed started indoors.

Epimedium x rubrum

COMMON NAME:

BARRENWORT

Family: Berberidaceae
Hardiness: Zones 5–8
Shade Tolerance/Preference: Light, partial, or full shade

Habit and Mature Size: Barrenwort grows 8 to 12 inches (20.5 to 30.5cm) tall in a lush mound and spreads very slowly by underground stems.

Aesthetic Value: The flowers of barrenwort are held on long stems and are crimson red with white spurs. They appear in spring and may be somewhat hidden by the foliage. Leaves are bright green with red margins and veins and they are outstanding in the summer and autumn. If the winter is mild, the foliage is semi-evergreen.

Cultural Needs: Barrenwort will thive in moist, humus-rich soil. Once it is established, it is extremely resilient and drought-tolerant. Cut the old foliage back to the

85

ground in early spring (it usually looks bedraggled after the winter). The new leaves will emerge with or just after the flowers.

Landscape Uses: This is a distinctive groundcover even though it does take some time to establish itself. It is also quite nice planted in the front of a perennial bed or along a shady path. It is lovely planted near ferns.

Insects and Diseases: Barrenwort has no serious pests or diseases.

Galium odoratum

COMMON NAMES:
SWEET WOODRUFF, BEDSTRAW

Family: Rubiaceae
Hardiness: Zones 4–8
Shade Tolerance/Preference: Light, partial, or full shade

Habit and Mature Size: Sweet woodruff grows 6 to 8 inches (15 to 20.5cm) tall and spreads over time to form a lush green carpet.

Aesthetic Value: Sweet woodruff is an excellent ground-cover, attractive throughout the growing season. Its emerald green leaves are held in loose whorls and when crushed or stepped upon smell like new-mown hay. In spring, tiny, pure white flowers clustered on erect stems blanket the plants.

Galium odoratum

Cultural Needs: This is a tough plant but it does require evenly moist, well-drained soil. It creeps slowly to form broad clumps and should be planted where it can be allowed to spread.

Landscape Uses: Sweet woodruff is a good choice for a groundcover under the high shade of deciduous trees if the site is not too dry. It is lovely along the edge of a woodland, especially if planted with spring bulbs and other shade-loving wildflowers.

Insects and Diseases: This plant has no serious pests or diseases.

Helleborus orientalis

COMMON NAME:
LENTEN ROSE

Family: Ranunculaceae
Hardiness: Zones 5–8
Shade Tolerance/Preference:
Light, partial, or full (but deciduous) shade

Habit and Mature Size: Lenten rose grows up to 2 feet (61cm) in a rounded clump.

Aesthetic Value: Lenten rose has very large, palmately divided, lustrous green leaves that are extremely showy. The foliage is evergreen. The flowers appear beginning in February or March and are glorious. Each stalk holds several cup-shaped nodding flowers in shades of creamy white, pink, pale lavender, or chartreuse fading to chocolate brown. The inside part of the flower is often speckled.

Cultural Needs: Plant Lenten rose in rich, moist, well-drained soil with plenty of organic matter added.

Landscape Uses: This is a wonderful plant to naturalize under deciduous trees and shrubs. Combine Lenten roses with early-flowering shrubs like corylopsis and *Rhododendron mucronulatum* or with daffodils, tulips, and other spring bulbs. The cut flowers of Lenten rose will bloom for weeks indoors.

Insects and Diseases: Lenten rose has no serious pests or diseases.

Helleborus orientalis

Helleborus foetidus

Other Species: *Helleborus foetidus* (Stinking hellebore) has numerous clusters of drooping, bell-shaped chartreuse flowers that hang just above the bottle green leaves. The flowers become rimmed with purple as they mature. What is most extraordinary about the flowers is they begin to bloom in mid-January and continue until March. Even when not in flower, this is an appealing plant because of its strong, evergreen leaves and intriguing form. Zones 6–8.

88

Heuchera sanguinea

COMMON NAME:
CORALBELLS

Family: Saxifragaceae / **Hardiness:** Zones 3–8
Shade Tolerance/Preference: Light or partial shade

Habit and Mature Size: This perennial forms a 4- to 6-inch (10 to 15cm) clump of leaves at the base. Its slender flower stalks rise a foot or two (30.5 to 61cm) above the foliage.

Heuchera sanguinea

Aesthetic Value: This species of heuchera is grown primarily for its flowers; other species are better known for their interesting foliage. Beginning in late April, *H. sanguinea* has tiny, bell-shaped flowers held on long, thin stems. The flower color will vary by cultivar, for the cultivars are more widely grown than the species. The colors range from white to chartreuse to pink and red and are enjoyed by hummingbirds. The leaves are small and round and may be evergreen in mild winters.

Cultural Needs: Coralbells like a fertile soil and demand good drainage, especially in winter. They will perform best if lifted and divided every three to four years. Remove old flower stalks to encourage further blooms. In the northernmost range of their hardiness, they should be covered with evergreen boughs in winter to keep them from heaving out of the ground after alternate freezing and thawing.

Landscape Uses: Their long-blooming and diminutive nature make these plants ideal for the edge of a path, for a rock garden, in the front of a perennial border, or in a rock wall. The delicate flower sprays are lovely in arrangements.

Insects and Diseases: Proper drainage will minimize problems, but some potential difficulties include powdery mildew, leaf spots, stem rot, and strawberry root weevil.

Cultivars: Most are from hybrids of *H. sanguinea* and *H. micrantha*: 'Chatterbox' grows 18 inches (46cm) tall and has rose-pink flowers; 'Firebird' matures at 15 inches (38cm) and has deep scarlet blooms. 'June Bride' has large white flowers and grows 18 inches (46cm) tall.

Hosta fortunei

COMMON NAME:
FORTUNE'S HOSTA

Family: Liliaceae / **Hardiness:** Zones 3–8
Shade Tolerance/Preference: Light or partial shade

Habit and Mature Size: The species and its cultivars are large plants with long, heart-shaped leaves. They tend to form 2-foot (61cm)-wide clumps. The flower stalks (known as scapes) grow 3 to 4 feet (1 to 1.2m) above the foliage. The overall habit is bold and dense.

Aesthetic Value: This is one of the preeminent species of hostas because of its grand leaves, which can be up to 12 inches (30.5cm) long and 6 to 8 inches (15 to 20.5cm) wide. The leaves of the species are grayish green and emerge late in the spring. Characteristic of this species are winged leaf stalks (known as petioles) up to 14 inches (35.5cm) long. The flowers are arranged in racemes and held aloft on tall scapes; the flowers are pale lilac and funnel-shaped.

Cultural Needs: This and other hostas like moist, well-drained soil and good air circulation. The primary factor in growing healthy hostas is maintaining a consistently moist (but not soggy) soil. Do not overfertilize and avoid nitrogen-rich fertilizers in particular.

Landscape Uses: A shady garden without hostas is unimaginable. Depending on the cultivar, hostas can be used as a single specimen in a perennial or shrub border or planted en masse as a groundcover under a deciduous

Hosta fortunei 'Aurea Marginata'

tree or alongside a northern or eastern wall. They are most effective when used in combination with plants that have markedly contrasting foliage, like ferns, astilbes, or sedges. The large-leaved forms are not only beautiful but practical as well—if carefully sited they are able to mask the unattractive dying foliage of spring bulbs.

Insects and Diseases: Slugs, aphids, and black vine weevils may all infest hostas.

Cultivars: 'Aurea' is smaller than the species. The new leaves are pale yellow with a cream-colored margin and they turn light green in summer. 'Francee' is one of the most popular hostas. It has dark green, heart-shaped leaves with a consistent white border. 'Gold Standard' has pale golden leaves edged in green. 'Hyacintha' has large, grayish green leaves.

Hosta sieboldiana

COMMON NAME:

SIEBOLD'S HOSTA

Family: Liliaceae
Hardiness: Zones 3–8
Shade Tolerance/Preference: Partial or light shade

Habit and Mature Size: This is one of the larger species of hosta, growing in clumps 2 to 3 feet (61cm to 1m) tall and 3 to 4 feet (1 to 1.2m) wide.

Aesthetic Value: Siebold's hosta and its cultivars are exceedingly beautiful. They have bluish green, heart-shaped leaves and pale lilac flowers held just slightly above the foliage. Some of the cultivars have attractively puckered leaves.

Cultural Needs: Like other hostas, Siebold's hosta likes moist, well-drained soil and good air circulation. The primary factor in growing healthy hostas is maintaining a consistently moist (but not soggy) soil. Do not overfertilize and avoid nitrogen-rich fertilizers in particular.

Landscape Uses: Plant Siebold's hosta as a single specimen in a perennial or shrub border or plant it en masse as a groundcover under a deciduous tree or along a northern or eastern wall. They are most effective when used in combination with plants that have markedly con-

trasting foliage, like ferns, astilbes, or sedges. If carefully sited they are able to mask the unattractive dying foliage of spring bulbs.

Insects and Diseases: Slugs, aphids, and black vine weevils may all infest hostas.

Cultivars: 'Aurora Borealis' grows 4 to 5 feet (1.2 to 1.5m) wide and has gold markings on bluish green leaves. 'Elegans' has been popular for almost a century. It has steely blue, puckered leaves and pale violet to white flowers. 'Frances Williams' has also been around for a long time for good reason. Its large, blue-green leaves have a striking golden margin. This is a particularly vigorous plant.

More than 400 hosta hybrids and cultivars exist, many of which were created only in the past ten years. A complete listing would be difficult and confusing, but there are several forms I am especially fond of: 'Antioch' has large green leaves with a broad, cream-colored margin. 'Aphrodite' is a real jewel with double white, very fragrant flowers. 'Blue Umbrellas' has gigantic, heavily puckered, deep blue-green leaves. 'Ginko Craig' has long, narrow green leaves with an irregular white edge and purple flowers. It grows only 18 inches (46cm) tall. 'Halcyon' grows about 2 feet (61cm) tall and has spear-shaped, chalky blue leaves. 'Kabitan' has long, narrow golden leaves with an uneven green margin. 'Krossa Regal' has large, oval, powder blue leaves and very tall scapes with lavender flowers. 'Patriot' has forest green leaves with a wide, uneven white margin. 'Sum and Substance' has massive, yellow-green leaves and pale lavender flowers. This is an outstanding specimen plant.

Iris cristata

COMMON NAMES:

CRESTED IRIS, DWARF CRESTED IRIS

Family: Iridaceae
Hardiness: Zones 3–9
Shade Tolerance/Preference:
Light or partial shade

Habit and Mature Size: Crested iris grows 4 to 8 inches (10 to 20.5cm) tall and spreads widely but not rapidly by creeping rhizomes.

Iris cristata

Aesthetic Value: The short, broad leaves of crested Iris are arranged in fans and tend to elongate after flowering is completed. The foliage is attractive throughout the growing season. In early or midspring, sky blue flowers, with a yellow and white patch or crest in the center, appear just barely above the leaves.

Cultural Needs: Well-drained soil with leaf mold added is ideal for these native plants. Overly fertilized soil will encourage vegetative growth at the expense of flowers. Sharp drainage is the most critical factor. When planting, leave the rhizome slightly exposed with the leaves pointing in the direction the plant should grow.

Landscape Uses: Plant crested iris as a groundcover on a partly shady hillside or slope for best effect. It is also nice along a wooded path or in a rock garden.

Insects and Diseases: Slugs, iris borer, aphids, and thrips may all pose problems for the crested iris.

Cultivars: 'Alba' has pure white flowers with a yellow crest. 'Summer Storm' has rich, deep blue flowers. 'Vein Mountain' has broad leaves and pale blue flowers with an orange crest outlined in purple.

Iris sibirica

COMMON NAME:

SIBERIAN IRIS

Family: Iridaceae

Hardiness: Zones 4–9

Shade Tolerance/Preference:

Light or partial shade or full sun

Habit and Mature Size: Siberian irises form graceful clumps and grow about 3 feet (1m) tall.

Aesthetic Value: This is one of the most elegant species of iris. It has tall, narrow, slightly arching leaves that are handsome throughout the growing season. In May and June numerous blue or violet flowers arise on strong, hollow stems. Later in the season attractive brown seed-pods, useful in dried arrangements, appear.

Cultural Needs: Siberian iris likes a fertile, moist soil with a neutral pH but it will certainly manage in less than ideal conditions. Plants should be fertilized lightly in the spring and watered deeply during dry spells.

Iris sibirica

Divide the clumps in spring or autumn every three or four years to ensure optimum flowering and overall plant vigor.

Landscape Uses: Their persistently vertical and attractive leaves make these plants exceptionally valuable in a cottage garden or mixed border. They are exquisite combined with roses, peonies, or poppies. Plant them in groups alongside a pond or stream—the reflection of their blossoms in the water is breathtaking.

Insects and Diseases: Borers and iris weevil are occasionally a problem.

Cultivars: 'Ego' has blue, bicolored flowers and excellent foliage. 'Eric the Red' has reddish purple flowers. 'Mountain Lake' has clear blue flowers on strong stems. 'My Love' has sky blue flowers and tends to rebloom. 'Persimmon' has midnight blue flowers. 'White Swirl' is a tall-growing form with white flowers with a yellow throat.

Lamiastrum galeobdolon

COMMON NAME:

YELLOW ARCHANGEL

Family: Labiatae

Hardiness: Zones 4–9

Shade Tolerance/Preference:

Partial to full shade

Habit and Mature Size: Yellow archangel grows only 8 to 14 inches (20.5 to 35.5cm) tall but spreads very rapidly to cover an area. It is a thug of a plant with a rampant habit but useful in certain situations.

Aesthetic Value: The leaves of this plant are rather appealing. They are oval to triangular in shape and are spotted with silver markings. The yellow flowers appear in spring in whorls in the axils of the upper leaves. The cultivars are more ornamental than the species. Where winters are mild the foliage is evergreen.

Cultural Needs: Yellow archangel will tolerate, even thrive, in almost any soil. It prefers rich, well-drained soil but will perform perfectly well in a dry, infertile site. Cut back the flowers after they bloom to keep the plants tidy.

Lamiastrum galeobdolon

Landscape Uses: Use this plant carefully because it will spread aggressively. In a difficult spot where a tough, rapidly spreading ground cover is needed it is ideal.

Insects and Diseases: Slugs and snails may infest yellow archangel.

Cultivars: 'Herman's Pride' is smaller in size and form than the species. It has dark green leaves flecked with silver and grows only 8 inches (20.5cm) tall. 'Variegatum' has leaves that are mainly silver with green midribs and margins.

Lamium maculatum

COMMON NAME:

SPOTTED DEAD NETTLE

Family: Labiatae

Hardiness: Zones 3–8

Shade Tolerance/Preference:

Light or partial shade

Habit and Mature Size: This is a creeping, spreading groundcover that grows 6 to 12 inches (15 to 30.5cm) tall. The species is invasive but the cultivars are more restrained.

Lamium maculatum

Aesthetic Value: The leaves of spotted dead nettle are compact and have a prominent silver or white stripe down the center. The stems are square, typical of members of the mint family. The flowers in spring are rosy pink.

Cultural Needs: Prefers a moist, well-drained soil rich in organic matter but will tolerate relatively difficult conditions. Cut the plants back after flowering to keep them neat and compact.

Landscape Uses: Plant the species with care, since it can spread with abandon, but the cultivars of *Lamium maculatum* are quite attractive and are ideal as a groundcover under evergreens or deciduous trees or shrubs. Plant them in groups and combine them with spring-flowering bulbs.

Insects and Diseases: Slugs may present a problem for spotted dead nettle.

Cultivars: 'Album' has green and white leaves and creamy white flowers. 'Beacon Silver' is a popular form with rose-colored flowers and silver leaves outlined in green. It is less hardy than the species. 'White Nancy' is similar in form to 'Beacon Silver' but has bright white flowers.

Ligularia stenocephala *'The Rocket'*

COMMON NAME:
ROCKET LIGULARIA

Family: Compositae
Hardienss: Zones 4–8
Shade Tolerance/Preference: Light or partial shade

Habit and Mature Size: This is a bold plant that grows 3 to 4 feet (1 to 1.2m) tall and 2 to 3 feet (61cm to 1m) wide.

Aesthetic Value: This intriguing plant has deeply lobed triangle-shaped leaves up to 1 foot (30.5cm) long. The

Ligularia stenocephala 'The Rocket'

ems are a rich, blackish purple and very dramatic against the tall, slender spikes of golden yellow flowers in summer.

Cultural Needs: Ligularias like an evenly moist soil and will wilt in dry conditions or afternoon sun. They rarely need division and prefer a cool climate.

Landscape Uses: This is a satisfying plant in a perennial or mixed border for its strong foliage and its showy, upright flowers. Ligularias can also be splendid planted in a group along a stream or pond where they are sure to receive the moisture they demand. Other forms of ligularia, notably *L. dentata*, are grown more for their spectacular foliage than for their flowers—look for the cultivars 'Desdemona' and 'Othello' in particular.

Insects and Diseases: Slugs and snails are potential pests.

Liriope muscari

COMMON NAME:

BIG BLUE LILYTURF

Family: Liliaceae
Hardiness: Zones 6–9
Shade Tolerance/Preference:
Full sun or light, partial, or full shade

Habit and Mature Size: This perennial forms tufted clumps of arching, straplike leaves and grows 12 to 18 inches (30.5 to 46cm) tall.

Aesthetic Value: Lilyturf is widely used because of its reliably evergreen leaves and dense whorls of lilac-purple flower spikes in late summer. The flowers are followed by shiny black fruits that perist into winter.

Cultural Needs: Lilyturf prefers moist, fertile, well-drained soil but will manage in less than ideal conditions. This is a plant that is hard to kill. It is remarkably tolerant of heat, high humidity, and drought, which explains why it is so popular in the southern United States. In cooler climates, the foliage looks battered after the winter and should be mowed to the ground in early spring. Lilyturf can be dug up and divided any time of year to create more plants.

Liriope muscari

Landscape Uses: Big blue lilyturf is an extraordinarily versatile plant, though it is clearly overused in certain regions. It makes a fine edging along a path and is a resilient groundcover for underplanting beneath trees and shrubs.

Insects and Diseases: Lilyturf has no serious pests or diseases.

Cultivars: 'John Birch' grows 18 inches (46cm) high and forms a thick mat of arching green leaves with creamy white margins. 'Lilac Beauty' has lilac flowers held high above deep green, grasslike leaves. 'Munroe's White' has white flower spikes and green leaves.

Lobelia cardinalis

COMMON NAME:
CARDINAL FLOWER

Family: Lobeliaceae
Hardiness: Zones 3–9
Shade Tolerance/Preference:
Light or partial shade

Habit and Mature Size: Cardinal flowers form rosettes of leaves that stay green all winter. Sturdy, erect stems rise above these foliage clumps to an ultimate height of 2 to 4 feet (61cm to 1.2m).

Aesthetic Value: In late summer, the shady garden is illuminated by the fiery red flower spikes of cardinal flower. These scarlet spikes rise 2 feet (61cm) above the leaves and are much loved by hummingbirds. The flowering persists for two or three weeks and is followed by the formation of tiny seed capsules.

Cultural Needs: Cardinal flowers are native to wet, boggy sites and they demand an evenly moist soil. It is wise to mulch them during the growing season and to provide winter protection in cold climates. Cardinal flowers do tend to be short-lived and usually last only two or three years in a garden setting.

Landscape Uses: Cardinal flowers are most attractive planted in groups alongside ponds and streams and allowed to naturalize. They combine well with other moisture-loving perennials like monkshood, helenium, and Siberian or Japanese iris. A smaller planting of cardinal flowers in a mixed border can also be effective, but the plants are not likely to be as long-lived here.

Insects and Diseases: Cardinal flower has no serious pests or diseases.

Other species: *Lobelia splendens* (Mexican lobelia) is a related species which is often sold as *L. cardinalis*. Beware of this confusion, because Mexican lobelia, while larger and more colorful than cardinal flower, is not as tolerant of cold weather or dry soils, and is likely to be much shorter-lived. To Zone 8.

Pachysandra terminalis

COMMON NAME:
JAPANESE SPURGE

Family: Buxaceae
Hardiness: To Zone 5
Shade Tolerance/Preference:
Light, partial, or full shade

Habit and Mature Size: Japanese spurge grows 6 to 8 inches (15 to 20.5cm) high and eventually forms a dense groundcover.

Aesthetic Value: Thick, dark green, spoon-shaped leaves make this an attractive plant year-round. Greenish white flower spikes rise above the leaves in spring and are followed by small, white, oval berries.

Cultural Needs: Pachysandra will perform best in moist, neutral, well-drained soil. In too much sun or overly dry conditions the foliage will yellow.

Landscape Uses: This plant is terribly overused but persistently attractive and a tough groundcover. It fills in relatively quickly and is able to tolerate sites that most other plants would find inhospitable.

Insects and Diseases: Leaf blight may pose a problem.

Cultivars: 'Green Carpet' has lower-growing, deeper green leaves than the species. 'Variegata' (a.k.a. 'Silver Edge') has green and cream-colored variegated leaves but is not as robust as the species.

Pachysandra terminalis

Phlox divaricata

COMMON NAMES:

WILD BLUE PHLOX, WOODLAND PHLOX

Family: Polemoniaceae

Hardiness: Zones 3–9

Shade Tolerance/Preference:
Light, partial, or full (but deciduous) shade

Habit and Mature Size: This is a low, creeping species of phlox that grows 12 to 15 inches (30.5 to 38cm) tall and spreads to form an appealing groundcover.

Aesthetic Value: While this species is not as showy as the sun-loving summer phlox (*P. paniculata*), it is charming in a quiet manner. It has dark green, oblong leaves that weave their way here and there through other plants in the garden. In spring, pale blue flowers are held in clusters above sticky, slender stems. The stalks wither after flowering and a clear green mat of foliage remains through the season.

Cultural Needs: Wild blue phlox is native to eastern woodlands and favors an evenly moist soil rich in organic matter. Removal of faded flowers will encourage the growth of new foliage.

Landscape Uses: Wild blue phlox is wonderful in a shady wildflower garden where its delicate blue flowers combine perfectly with spring bulbs and other early bloomers like Virginia bluebells, bleeding-hearts, and foamflower. Use it also in the shade of deciduous trees to underplant hostas and other taller-growing plants or along a woodland path.

Insects and Diseases: Rabbits can be a nuisance and powdery mildew is sometimes a problem in hot, humid climates.

Cultivars: 'Dirgo Ice' has icy blue flowers and narrow leaves. 'Fuller's White' has pure white flowers. 'Lamphamii' has deep blue blooms with full, notchless petals. 'London Grove' has fragrant violet-blue flowers in exceptionally large clusters. 'Louisiana' grows to about 6 inches (15cm) in height, and bears purple-blue flowers earlier in spring than other cultivars.

Polygonatum biflorum

COMMON NAME:

SMALL SOLOMON'S SEAL

Family: Liliaceae

Hardiness: Zones 3–9

Shade Tolerance/Preference: Partial to full shade

Habit and Mature Size: This native plant grows 2 to 3 feet (61cm to 1m) tall and has a gracefully elegant, arching habit.

Aesthetic Value: The form, foliage, and flowers of Solomon's seal are thoroughly engaging. The arching stems bear clear green, oval leaves in an alternate pattern that

Polygonatum biflorum

gives a sense of ascending a stairway. In spring bell-shaped, greenish white flowers dangle airily in clusters from the leaf axils—the overall effect is quite magical.

Cultural Needs: Solomon's seal prefers a moist, humus-rich soil but is very tolerant of dry conditions. It spreads by branching rhizomes and should be lifted and divided whenever it seems to have overgrown its site. Division is easiest in the spring.

Landscape Uses: Plant this perennial in naturalized woodlands, in a shady perennial or shrub border, or even in the dry shade of a mature deciduous tree.

Insects and Diseases: Solomon's seal has no serious pests or diseases.

Primula japonica

COMMON NAME:

JAPANESE PRIMROSE

Family: Primulaceae

Hardiness: Zones 5–7

Shade Tolerance/Preference: Light or partial shade

Habit and Mature Size: Japanese primrose grows 1 to 2 feet (30.5 to 61cm) tall.

Aesthetic Value: This is one of the "candelabra" primroses, so named because its flower stems hold two to six whorls of flowers and each whorl in turn consists of eight to twelve flowers. The flowers bloom in June and July

97

Primula japonica

in shades of pink, rose, or white. The leaves of this species are broad, paddle-shaped, and concentrated at the base of the plant.

Cultural Needs: Japanese primrose requires a cool, constantly moist, almost boggy soil that is rich in organic matter. In cold climates a winter mulch is necessary; in warm climates the plants must be protected from afternoon sun. Overgrown plants should be dug up and divided after flowering.

Landscape Uses: This plant is superb in a consistently moist perennial bed or if allowed to naturalize beside a pond or stream along with Japanese or Siberian irises and astilbes.

Insects and Diseases: Slugs, snails, and red spider mites may all infest Japanese primroses.

Cultivars: 'Miller's Crimson' has rich, red flowers. 'Postford White' has multiple whorls of large white flowers.

Other Species: *Primula denticulata* (drumstick primose) has long, spatula-shaped leaves with sharply toothed margins. From the center of the leaves a thick stalk rises in May and June, crowned by a dense cluster of white or lavender flowers. Zones 4–8.

Pulmonaria saccharata

COMMON NAME:
BETHLEHEM SAGE

Family: Boraginaceae
Hardiness: Zones 3–8
Shade Tolerance/Preference:
Partial to full shade

Habit and Mature Size: Bethlehem sage forms a compact clump 9 to 18 inches (23 to 46cm) tall with leaves 6 to 12 inches (15 to 30.5cm) wide.

Primula denticulata

Pulmonaria saccharata

Aesthetic Value: Bethlehem sage blooms in early spring with clusters of pink buds that open to reveal violet-blue flowers. The foliage is pale green with handsome silver spots. Even though the plant does not flower prolifically, the unusual foliage is reason enough to grow it.

Cultural Needs: Bethlehem sage needs an evenly moist soil rich in organic material and prefers cool temperatures. In the heat of summer it tends to languish. When the clumps become overgrown lift and divide them either in spring or autumn.

Landscape Uses: This and other species of Pulmonaria are lovely planted with other spring-blooming perennials and bulbs in the front of a perennial border, along a shady path, or on the edge of a woodland garden. Their dappled foliage is very nice against plants with darker, solid-colored leaves like ophiopogon and hellebore.

Insects and Diseases: Slugs are occasionally a problem and some of the older forms are prone to powdery mildew if air circulation is inadequate.

Cultivars: 'Boughton Blue' has clear blue flowers atop leaves with silver-gray blotches. 'Janet Fisk' has lavender-pink flowers and particularly dense spotted leaves. 'Mrs. Moon' has flowers that are pink when they open and later fade to blue. The leaves are broad with silver speckles.

Tiarella cordifolia

COMMON NAME:

ALLEGHENY FOAMFLOWER

Family: Saxifragaceae

Hardiness: Zones 3–8

Shade Tolerance/Preference:

Partial or full shade

Habit and Mature Size: Foamflower grows 6 to 10 inches (15 to 25.5cm) tall in a neat mound. It spreads via slender trailing stems and eventually forms a dense groundcover.

Aesthetic Value: The leaves of foamflower are heart-shaped and slightly crinkled. It has purplish veins that are very prominent in winter and spring. In May and June

Tiarella cordifolia

clusters of tiny, star-shaped, pale pink to white flowers are held on 3- to 4-inch (7.5 to 10cm) long arching stems.

Cultural Needs: Foamflower likes a cool climate and thrives in moist soil rich in organic matter. In prolonged dry spells it appears to go dormant. Plants can be lifted and divided in spring or autumn and rooted runners can be dug and replanted anytime during the growing season.

Landscape Uses: Allegheny foamflower makes a fine groundcover planted in groups in evenly moist soil in a shady site. If the soil is not too dry, it will perform well under trees or shrubs and is especially attractive planted with spring bulbs, columbines, trilliums, or woodland phlox.

Insects and Diseases: Allegheny foamflower has no serious pests or diseases.

Cultivars: 'Dunvegan' grows 6 inches (15cm) tall and has pink flowers and deeply dissected leaves with outstanding autumn color. 'Oakleaf' has pale pinkish white flowers and oak-shaped leaves.

Tricyrtis hirta

COMMON NAME:

COMMON TOAD LILY

Family: Liliaceae / **Hardiness:** Zones 4–9
Shade Tolerance/Preference: Light or partial shade

Habit and Mature Size: Common toad lily forms a 3-foot (1m) tall upright and open clump.

Aesthetic Value: Toad lilies bloom late in the season, usually at the very end of summer or in early autumn. Their flowers are both beautiful and structurally complex. They are funnel-shaped and upward-facing and form in the leaf axils along the 2- to 3-foot (61cm to 1m) arching stems. The flowers are white with purple and black spots. The leaves of this species are deep green and broadly lance-shaped.

Cultural Needs: Toad lilies will thrive in consistently moist soil rich in humus. In hot, dry weather they should

Tricyrtis hirta

be mulched and may need supplemental watering. They resent being moved, so try to plant them where they can remain undisturbed. In cool climates plant toad lilies in a bit more sun to encourage flowering before frost.

Landscape Uses: Toad lilies are best planted where you can appreciate their lovely and intricate flowers at close range. Site them along a shady path or on the edge of a woodland garden or toward the front of a perennial border.

Insects and Diseases: Toad lily has no serious pests or diseases.

Trillium grandiflorum

COMMON NAMES:

WHITE TRILLIUM, SNOW TRILLIUM

Family: Liliaceae
Hardiness: Zones 3–9
Shade Tolerance/Preference:
Partial or full shade

Habit and Mature Size: Grows 1 to 2 feet (30.5 to 61cm) tall with leaves 4 to 6 inches (10 to 15cm) long.

Aesthetic Value: White trillium is a classic eastern woodland plant. In spring wide, snowy white flowers stand up above the broad, bright green leaves. The flowers are wavy and slightly nodding and fade over time to pale rose pink. Round berries appear after flowering and by mid- to late summer the plants go dormant if the weather is warm and dry.

Cultural Needs: Trilliums should be planted in evenly moist soil rich in organic matter. They prefer a cool climate and will colonize in a hospitable site. Buy only nursery-propagated plants from reputable dealers and do not collect plants from the wild.

Landscape Uses: Trilliums are perfect for shady wildflower gardens, combined, for instance, with ferns, Solomon's seal, or wild blue phlox. Underplant trees and shrubs with them and mix in flowering bulbs for an entrancing springtime composition.

Insects and Diseases: White trillium has no serious pests or diseases.

Trillium grandiflorum

Vinca minor

COMMON NAME:
COMMON PERIWINKLE

Family: Apocynaceae
Hardiness: Zones 4–9
Shade Tolerance/Preference:
Light, partial, or full shade.

Habit and Mature Size: Grows 4 to 6 inches (10 to 15cm) tall and slowly runs to form a dense mat.

Aesthetic Value: This is one of the toughest and hardiest evergreen ground covers for shade. It is attractive as well, with dark green oval leaves and small, light blue flowers in the spring.

Cultural Needs: Periwinkle is undemanding but prefers average, well-drained soil that is neither too wet nor too dry. The runners should be periodically cut back to keep the plants looking lush and full.

Landscape Uses: This is a carefree and appealing ground cover under trees and shrubs. It is also attractive allowed to trail over and down a wall.

Insects and Diseases: Periwinkle has no serious pests or diseases.

Vinca minor

ANNUALS

Coleus

Ageratum houstonianum

COMMON NAMES:
COMMON AGERATUM, FLOSSFLOWER

Family: Compositae
Shade Tolerance/Preference: Light shade

Habit and Mature Size: Size will vary by cultivar. The short forms are 5 to 9 inches (12.5 to 23cm) tall and the taller cultivars grow 24 to 30 inches (61 to 76cm).

Aesthetic Value: Ageratums are covered from late spring until frost in dense clusters of lavender-blue flowers. The flowers are daisylike but without the usual ray flowers, or petals, that are characteristic of members of this family. The foliage is pale green and rather coarse.

Cultural Needs: Ageratums like a moist, rich soil and warm weather. Set the plants out after all danger of frost has passed and they will flower relentlessly through summer and autumn. Try to periodically pinch off the spent blooms to encourage further flowering and bushier plants.

Landscape Uses: This plant is excellent in containers, along a path, in the front of a mixed border, or as an edging plant.

Insects and Diseases: Ageratums have no serious pests or diseases.

Cultivars: 'Blue Danube' grows 6 to 8 inches (15 to 20.5cm) tall and has lavender-blue flowers. 'Blue Horizon' grows 30 inches (76cm) high and its flowers are good for cutting. 'Pink Powderpuff' is a dwarf form with pink flowers. 'Summer Snow' has white flowers and stays 6 to 8 inches (15 to 20.5cm) tall.

Begonia x semperflorens-cultorum

COMMON NAME:
WAX BEGONIA

Family: Begoniaceae
Shade Tolerance/Preference Light or partial shade

Habit and Mature Size: Size will vary by cultivar, but these plants generally grow 8 to 12 inches (20.5 to 30.5cm) tall with a few forms growing to 16 inches (40.5cm).

Aesthetic Value: The flowers of wax begonia will be, depending upon the cultivar, in shades of pink, white, rose, or red. The foliage is either bright green or bronze. The plants bloom continuously from late spring until frost.

Ageratum houstonianum *'Blue Horizon'*

Begonia x semperflorens-cultorum

Cultural Needs: Begonias like a well-fertilized soil that is evenly moist. Good air circulation and protection from the hot summer sun will help ensure healthy plants.

Landscape Uses: This is a lovely plant for containers, edging, or the front of a mixed border. If you bring wax begonias inside before frost they make colorful house-plants.

Insects and Diseases: Whiteflies, mealybugs, leaf spot, and gray mold may all affect wax begonias.

Cultivars: 'Cocktail Mix' grows 6 to 8 inches (15 to 20.5cm) tall and has mixed flower colors and bronze foliage. 'Gin' has white flowers and bronze leaves.

Browallia speciosa

COMMON NAME:
AMETHYST FLOWER

Family: Solanaceae

Shade Tolerance/Preference: Light or partial shade

Habit and Mature Size: Grows 10 to 18 inches (25.5 to 46cm) high.

Aesthetic Value: Amethyst flower has blue, somewhat trailing flowers that make this plant ideal for hanging baskets on a shady porch. The flowers are star-shaped and the plants tend to be extremely free-flowering, especially if the weather is not too dry.

Cultural Needs: Amethyst flower thrives in warm, humid weather and in evenly moist soil. Pinch it back periodically to encourage flowering and maintain a compact shape.

Landscape Uses: This is an ideal plant for containers and hanging baskets. Amethyst flowers can be brought inside before frost and will bloom on and off through the winter if indoor temperatures do not fall below 55°F (13°C).

Insects and Diseases: Amethyst flower has no serious pests or diseases.

Cultivars: 'Blue Bells Improved' has violet-blue flowers and a bushy habit without pinching. 'Jingle Bells' is available in shades of blue, lavender, and white. 'White Troll' grows only 10 inches (25.5cm) high and has white flowers.

Browallia speciosa

Coleus x hybridus

COMMON NAME:
COLEUS

Family: Labiatae

Shade Tolerance/Preference:
Light, partial, or full shade

Habit and Mature Size: Varies widely by cultivar, but ranges from 6 to 36 inches (15cm to 1m).

Aesthetic Value: Coleus is grown for its vibrant foliage. Depending upon the cultivar, the leaves can be solid, bicolored, or multicolored; large or small; scalloped or smooth-edged; heart-shaped or oval; and on and on. Some cultivars branch from the base and need no pinching back, but others must be regularly pinched or they become leggy. The flowers are not showy and are best pinched off for bushier plants.

Cultural Needs: Coleus likes a moist, well-drained soil and warm temperatures.

Coleus x hybridus

Hypoestes phyllostachya

Landscape Uses: Depending on the form you choose, coleus is a good bedding plant and is effective in pots, as an edging, and under trees and shrubs. Cuttings taken before frost are easily overwintered indoors on a bright windowsill.

Insects and Diseases: Aphids, mealybugs, and whiteflies are all potential pests.

Cultivars: 'Kaleidoscope Jade' grows 6 to 12 inches (15 to 30.5cm) tall and has a spreading habit. The leaves are large and bright green with a clear yellow midrib. 'Poncho' cultivars were bred specifically for hanging baskets. 'Wizard Scarlet' branches from the base and demands no pinching to keep it bushy. The leaves are large and deep scarlet with a golden yellow outline.

Hypoestes phyllostachya

COMMON NAME:
POLKA-DOT PLANT

Family: Acanthaceae

Shade Tolerance/Preference:
Partial or full shade

Habit and Mature Size: 12 to 18 inches (30.5 to 46cm)

Aesthetic Value: Hypoestes is grown for its heart-shaped leaves, which are green and speckled with whitish pink dots. The leaves may grow as much as 4 inches (10cm) long and 2 inches (5cm) wide. Late in the season dark violet flowers appear.

Cultural Needs: Polka-dot plant prefers a moist soil rich in organic matter. Good drainage is essential. Seeds are easily started indoors and the plants should be pinched back when they are about 10 inches (25.5cm) high to promote bushiness. Set them out 6 to 10 inches (15 to 25.5cm) apart once there is no danger of frost.

Landscape Uses: The bright speckling of their leaves makes these engaging plants to use as a summer ground-cover under trees, in pots, or in the foreground of a mixed border. They also make fine houseplants.

Insects and Diseases: Polka-dot plant has no serious pests or diseases.

Cultivars: 'Pink Splash' has larger, deep pink spots. 'White Spalsh' has clear white dots against a green background.

Impatiens wallerana

COMMON NAME:
IMPATIENS

Family: Balsaminaceae

Shade Tolerance/Preference:
Light, partial, or full shade

Habit and Mature Size: Size varies by cultivar, but generally plants grow 1 to 2 feet (30.5 to 61cm) high.

Aesthetic Value: This is another one of those plants that is ubiquitous in North American gardens. It has become truly commonplace but is so long-blooming and so thoroughly carefree that it seems foolish not to grow it. What other plant will flower so profusely even in deep shade? The choice of flower colors is enormous—cultivars are available in shades of white, pink, red, orange, scarlet, apricot, bicolored, and in double or single flower forms, and so on.

Cultural Needs: Impatiens are native to a tropical climate and they will flower heavily once the weather is warm. They prefer a moist, well-drained soil and should be fertilized periodically throughout the growing season.

Landscape Uses: Impatiens are wonderful planted in pots, along a shady path, or in large groups beneath mature trees and shrubs—the possibilities are endless.

Insects and Diseases: White-tail deer are a problem.

Impatiens wallerana

Lobelia erinus

COMMON NAME:
EDGING LOBELIA

Family: Lobeliaceae

Shade Tolerance/Preference: Light or partial shade in warm climates; light shade or full sun in cool climates

Habit and Mature Size: Grows 4 to 8 inches (10 to 20,5cm) tall in either mounding or trailing forms.

Aesthetic Value: This is a charming plant as long as the weather is not too hot. Masses of tiny purple, blue, lilac, magenta, or white flowers envelop the greenish to bronze leaves. The colors are intense and make a strong show even on such diminutive plants.

Cultural Needs: Edging lobelia likes average to rich, moist soil. It should be sheared back to 2 inches (5cm) after the first blooms have faded to encourage continued vigorous flowering. Where summers are very hot, this plant is likely to stop flowering until the weather cools.

Landscape Uses: The vibrant flowers of edging lobelia are lovely in hanging pots and window boxes, in rock walls, and between paving stones.

Insects and Diseases: Edging lobelia has no serious pests or diseases.

Cultivars: 'Cascade' is a trailing form, excellent for handing baskets. 'Crystal Palace' has cobalt blue flowers and bronze leaves.

107

Lobelia erinus

Nicotiana langsdorfii

COMMON NAME:

NO COMMON NAME

Family: Solanaceae

Shade Tolerance/Preference:

Light or partial shade or full sun

Habit and Mature Size: *Nicotiana langsdorfii* grows 3 to 4 feet (1 to 1.2m) tall. It is much less coarse than other flowering tobaccos; indeed it is quite graceful and elegant in form and habit.

Aesthetic Value: The flowers of *N. langsdorfii* have an intriguing shape and a most unusual color. They are pale green, almost chartreuse, and they hang down from multiple wiry stems. The flowers look like narrow pendant bells and they are greatly favored by hummingbirds. The leaves are a soft, pale green and provide a perfect complement to the enchanting flowers.

Cultural Needs: This is an exceptionally undemanding plant. It is drought- and heat-tolerant and seems to require no deadheading or other attention. It may self-sow here and there, but not in an aggressive manner.

Nicotiana langsdorfii

Landscape Uses: The neutral color of its foliage and flowers make this an easy plant to integrate into a perennial or mixed border. Place it toward the front because one can easily see through its narrow stems. It is splendid along a path where its interesting flowers can be studied up close. The flowers are also beautiful in arrangements and will last for a week if cut before fully opened.

Insects and Diseases: *N. langsdorfii* has no serious pests or diseases.

Torenia fournieri

COMMON NAME:

WISHBONE FLOWER

Family: Scrophulariaceae

Shade Tolerance/Preference: Partial or full shade

Habit and Mature Size: Wishbone flower grows 8 to 10 inches (20.5 to 25.5cm) tall and about 6 inches (15cm) wide.

Aesthetic Value: The charms of wishbone flower are of a subtle nature. If you examine the flowers up close you will see in the center two wishbone-shaped stamens that touch at the tip. This is how the common name arose. The stamens spring apart when it is time for the flower to be pollinated. Flowers come in shades of deep rose, purple, light blue, dark blue, and white; they all have a yellow throat. The leaves are toothed along the edge and dark green in color.

Cultural Needs: Wishbone flower is native to the tropics and naturally prefers a warm, humid climate and evenly moist soil rich in organic matter. The flowers will quickly fade under dry conditions.

Landscape Uses: Wishbone flower makes an excellent bedding plant and is especially effective at the edge of a shady path or in a container. It can be brought inside and grown as a houseplant but will probably need frequent spraying with insecticidal soap to control the aphids and other pests that tend to plague it.

Insects and Diseases: Aphids and whiteflies.

Cultivars: 'Happy Faces' is a mixture of shades of plum, blue, pink, and white bicolor flowers. 'Suzy Wong' has bright yellow flowers with a purplish black throat.

Torenia fournieri

ORNAMENTAL GRASSES

Acorus gramineus 'Variegatus'

Acorus gramineus
'Variegatus'

COMMON NAME:

VARIEGATED JAPANESE SWEET FLAG

Family: Araceae

Hardiness: To Zone 6

Shade Tolerance/Preference: Light or partial shade

Habit and Mature Size: This finely textured member of the Arum family (this is not technically a grass but is included here because it is so like a grass) grows 10 to 12 inches (25.5 to 30.5cm) tall and forms a dense but narrow clump.

Aesthetic Value: Japanese sweet flag is grown for its interesting green and white striped leaves. The flowers are tiny and greenish in color.

Cultural Needs: Japanese sweet flag is native to Asia and will thrive in wet, marshy soil. The soil should ideally be well-drained but consistently moist. If grown in too much sun the leaves will yellow and dry out. Plants can be propagated by dividing the stout rootstock.

Landscape Uses: Japanese sweet flag is very handsome planted in groups along a pond or stream or other boggy site.

Insects and Diseases: Spider mites may infest plants.

Chasmanthium latifolium

COMMON NAMES:

SEA OATS, WILD OATS, RIVER OATS

Family: Gramineae

Hardiness: Zones 4–9

Shade Tolerance/Preference: Light or partial shade

Habit and Mature Size: Forms a restrained clump 3 feet (1m) tall and 2 to 3 feet (61cm to 1m) wide. Sea oats have a tendency to self-sow.

Aesthetic Value: In spring long and narrow purplish green leaves emerge and grow in a somewhat horizontal, bamboolike fashion. In summer open panicles of pendulous, flattened green spikelets appear above the foliage.

Chasmanthium latifolium

These spikelets look like oats, which is how the common name arose. Initially a luminous bottle green in color, the spikelets are a beautiful sight when backlit by the sun. They gradually change to reddish purple, then to a shiny copper, and finally to chocolate brown after frost. The sight and sound of the dried spikelets in the winter landscape is hauntingly beautiful. If you cut the spikelets while still green, they will retain their color when dried indoors.

Cultural Needs: Sea oats prefer a rich, evenly moist soil. In prolonged dry spells it may wilt if not watered. Self-sown seedlings can be easily dug up and removed or prevented by cutting off the spikelets before the seeds drop. The spikelets and old foliage should in any event be cut back to the ground in late winter or early spring before the new leaves begin to grow.

Landscape Uses: This is an excellent plant to allow to naturalize along the edge of a woodland garden. It also peforms well planted as a specimen or in groups in a seashore setting because of its tolerance of salt spray. Wherever it is planted, and even a pot is a possibility, sea oats will be interesting and attractive from midspring through the following winter.

Insects and Diseases: Sea oats have no serious pests or diseases.

Hakonechloa macra
'Aureola'

COMMON NAME:
GOLDEN VARIEGATED HAKONE GRASS

Family: Gramineae
Hardiness: To Zone 5 or 6
Shade Tolerance/Preference: Light or partial shade

Habit and Mature Size: Golden variegated hakone grass has a slowly spreading, gracefully arching habit. It grows about 18 inches (46cm) high and 2 or 3 feet (61cm or 1m) wide, though it takes a long time for it to reach its mature width.

Aesthetic Value: It is hard to imagine a more refined and stately plant than this. The new leaves emerge in mid- to late spring and are golden yellow with bright green, slen-

Hakonechloa macra *'Aureola'*

der, vertical stripes. In fall the foliage is tinged with shades of rosy pink and red and becomes attractively straw-colored after frost.

Cultural Needs: Hakone grass likes a light, well-drained, reasonably fertile soil. It prefers evenly moist conditions but has proven to be remarkably drought-tolerant. The fact that it performs well in dry shade would make it worth growing even if it were not so beautiful. Cut back the old foliage in late winter or early spring.

Landscape Uses: In Japan this grass is often used in pots and is an elegant container plant. It is also excellent planted en masse as a groundcover under high canopy deciduous trees or on a shady slope, used in a perennial border in combination with hostas and ferns, tucked into a rock wall, or planted atop a wall and allowed to gently cascade down.

Insects and Diseases: Golden variegated hakone grass has no serious pests or diseases.

Phalaris arundinacea *var.* picta

COMMON NAMES:

RIBBON GRASS, GARDENER'S GARTERS

Family: Gramineae

Hardiness: Zones 4–9

Shade Tolerance/Preference:

Light or partial shade

Habit and Mature Size: This is a grass that will run vigorously if allowed. It grows 2 to 3 feet (61cm to 1m) tall and is wide-spreading over time.

Aesthetic Value: This form of ribbon grass has long, elegantly tapered leaves that are striped green and creamy white. The new foliage in the spring often has a blush of pink. Soft, white, spiky flowers appear in midsummer and turn a pale brown. When frost arrives, the plants bleach to an attractive beige, providing enduring winter interest.

Cultural Needs: Ribbon grass prefers a moist, well-drained soil but will manage in less than ideal conditions. In a hot climate cut back the foliage in summer to encourage clean, new growth in the cooler days of autumn. Ribbon grass will tolerate wet conditions but does not perform well in drought.

Landscape Uses: This old-fashioned favorite makes a fine groundcover as long as your climate is neither too hot nor too dry. It is also effective for stabilizing a slope, especially alongside a pond or stream. Ribbon grass will even grow in shallow water. Avoid using it in a mixed or perennial border because of its invasive nature.

Insects and Diseases: Ribbon grass has no serious pests or diseases.

Cultivars: 'Dwarf Garters' is a more delicate and compact form.

Other species/cultivars: *Phalaris arundinacea* 'Feesey's Form' ('Feesey's Form' ribbon grass) is an excellent cultivar of the species. It has white-striped foliage tinged with pink; white flowers appear in midsummer.

Phalaris arundinacea *var.* picta

FERNS

Adiantum pedatum

Adiantum pedatum

COMMON NAME:

NORTHERN MAIDENHAIR FERN

Family: Polypodiaceae

Hardiness: To Zone 3

Shade Tolerance/Preference: Light or partial shade

Habit and Mature Size: Northern maidenhair fern grows 12 to 24 inches (30.5 to 61cm) tall and has a very open, lacy habit.

Aesthetic Value: Northern maidenhair fern has an open and delicate form and texture. Its lacy, fanlike leaves (known as fronds) are light to medium green and are arranged on shiny, wiry, black stalks.

Cultural Needs: This hardy fern must be kept moist at all times. It prefers a loose, well-drained soil rich in organic matter, but surely the most critical element is constant moisture. It grows from branching rhizomes just below the soil surface but does not spread quickly or aggressively.

Landscape Uses: This deciduous fern is daintily attractive from early spring well into fall. It should be planted in woodland wildflower gardens and is wonderful with spring-flowering bulbs. Its airy nature makes it a good plant to tuck into a shady corner of the garden or a small nook in a rock wall.

Insects and Diseases: Northern maidenhair fern has no serious pests or diseases.

Athyrium filix-femina

COMMON NAME:

LADY FERN

Family: Polypodiaceae

Hardiness: Zones 4–8

Shade Tolerance/Preference: Light, partial, or full shade

Habit and Mature Size: Lady fern grows 2 feet (61cm) tall.

Aesthetic Value: Lady ferns are light green in color and have wide, lacy, finely dissected fronds. They continue to

Athyrium filix-femina

send up new leaves until late summer and thus the plant looks fresh and vibrant long after many other ferns have begun to languish.

Cultural Needs: This is one of the easiest ferns to grow. It likes moist, humus-rich, well-drained soil and may need to be watered during prolonged dry spells. Once it is established, it is one of the more drought-tolerant ferns. The soil pH should be neutral to slightly acidic. If conditions are favorable, lady fern will spread, though not rapidly or invasively.

Landscape Uses: This fern is lovely planted in groups on the edge of a woodland garden or mixed into a shady perennial border. It makes a fine groundcover in the high shade of deciduous trees.

Insects and Diseases: Lady fern has no serious pests or diseases.

Cultivars: 'Frizelliae' has its leaflets arranged along a single petiole and is more open and delicate than the species.

115

Athyrium nipponicum pictum

COMMON NAME:

JAPANESE PAINTED FERN

Family: Polypodiaceae / **Hardiness:** Zones 4–8
Shade Tolerance/Preference: Light, partial, or full shade

Habit and Mature Size: Grows 12 to 18 inches (30.5 to 46cm) tall.

Aesthetic Value: This is one of the most popular and ornamental of ferns. Its new fronds are a soft, frosted gray with shades of purple and blue. A silver stripe down the center of the mature fronds looks as if it had been painted on, hence the common name. The stems are wine red and quite showy.

Cultural Needs: Japanese painted fern likes a rich, moist, well-drained soil that is neutral to slightly acidic. It should be well watered during dry periods.

A t h y r i u m   n i p p o n i c u m   p i c t u m

Landscape Uses: A patch of Japanese painted ferns growing on the edge of a woodland garden is a stunning sight. Their silvery leaves catch the light and enliven a dark area. They are excellent combined with dark green hostas, hellebores, or wild ginger and a specimen in a rock garden is eye-catching indeed.

Insects and Diseases: This fern has no serious pests or diseases.

Other species: *Athyrium thelypterioides* (silvery glade fern) is larger than its cousin, *A. nipponicum pictum*, growing 2 to 4 feet (60 to 120cm) tall. It thrives in damp woodland settings, and is particularly good for planting along shady streamsides. This fern is cherished for its attractive, silver-colored spring fronds.

Dennstaedtia punctilobula

COMMON NAME:

HAY-SCENTED FERN

Family: Polypodiaceae
Hardiness: Zones 3–8
Shade Tolerance/Preference:
Light, partial, or full shade or sun

Habit and Mature Size: Grows 10 to 12 inches (25.5 to 30.5cm) high.

Aesthetic Value: This fern has light green, sword-shaped leaves with finely cut edges. In autumn the leaves turn a coppery russet color. One of the most appealing features of this particular fern is the scent of new-mown hay when the fronds are crushed.

Cultural Needs: Hay-scented fern likes a slightly acidic, evenly moist soil. It spreads rapidly by rhizomes growing just below the soil surface and will form a dense stand if conditions are favorable. It is deciduous and turns brown in early autumn.

Landscape Uses: This is a good choice for a ground-cover, especially on a shady hillside. It is one of the tougher ferns and, once established, it will withstand prolonged periods of wet or dry weather.

Insects and Diseases: Snails and thrips are potential pests.

Matteuccia struthiopteris

Matteuccia struthiopteris

COMMON NAME:

OSTRICH FERN

Family: Polypodiaceae / **Hardiness:** Zones 3–7
Shade Tolerance/Preference: Light or partial shade

Habit and Mature Size: Grows 3 to 4 feet (1 to 1.2m) tall in favorable conditions.

Aesthetic Value: This is a boldly textured plant with tall, elegant fronds that resemble ostrich feathers. The leaves are dark green and lustrous and grow in great whorls. The black fertile fronds are highly valued in arrangements.

Cultural Needs: Ostrich fern is native to marshy areas and deltas of shallow streams and will thus perform best in moist soil. It can manage in drier conditions but will not be nearly as tall or vigorous. It spreads by a system of dense underground runners and can be very invasive.

Landscape Uses: Plant this robust fern either where its unrestrained growth is an asset, for example as a groundcover, or where you can control its aggressive spread. Its height and dark green color make it a good background plant.

Insects and Diseases: Ostrich fern has no serious pests or diseases.

Osmunda cinnamomea

COMMON NAME:
CINNAMON FERN

Family: Polypodiaceae
Hardiness: Zones 3–10
Shade Tolerance/Preference: Light or partial shade

Habit and Mature Size: This has a clump-forming habit and grows 3 feet (1m) tall in a garden setting and over 5 feet (1.5m) in the wild.

Aesthetic Value: This attractive native fern has light green leaves that surround the woolly, cinnamon-colored young fronds. The mature leaves are strong and erect and remain green all through the growing season. The fiddleheads (i.e., the young coiled leaves) are edible.

Cultural Needs: Cinnamon fern will grow best in a constantly moist and acidic soil. It spreads slowly.

Landscape Uses: This is another good vertical background plant, effective either singly or in groups in a shady perennial or mixed border as long as the soil is evenly moist. It is handsome planted in drifts along a woodland edge or as a lone specimen in the corner of a wall.

Insects and Diseases: Cinnamon fern has no serious pests or diseases.

Osmunda regalis

COMMON NAME:
ROYAL FERN

Family: Polypodiaceae
Hardiness: To Zone 2
Shade Tolerance/Preference: Light or partial shade

Habit and Mature Size: This has a distinctly upright habit and grows 4 feet (1.2m) high.

Aesthetic Value: The leaves of royal fern are reddish green when they first emerge and then change to deep green. The leaves can be very long—3 to 4 feet (1 to 1.2m), perhaps even 6 feet (1.8m) under ideal conditions.

Osmunda cinnamomea

Osmunda regalis

The leaves are widely spaced and give this fern a distinctive appearance. Royal fern grows slowly and circumferentially, that is, it grows in a ring around the original plant and forms a larger and larger circle of plants. In autumn the green fronds turn yellow and the spore cases are a rich, golden brown.

Cultural Needs: Royal fern likes a highly acidic, very wet soil. It is not at all tolerant of drought.

Landscape Uses: This makes an effective vertical accent in a shady perennial or mixed border. Use it in groups along a stream or pond or on the moist edge of a woodland garden.

Insects and Diseases: Royal fern has no serious pests or diseases.

Polystichum acrostichoides

COMMON NAME:

CHRISTMAS FERN

Family: Polypodiaceae

Hardiness: To Zone 3

Shade Tolerance/Preference:

Light, partial, or full shade or sun

Habit and Mature Size: Christmas fern grows 18 to 24 inches (46 to 61cm) tall and forms a compact clump.

Aesthetic Value: This is an evergreen fern with leathery, dark green fronds.

Cultural Needs: Christmas fern prefers a consistently moist, well-drained soil that is rich in organic matter. If grown with adequate moisture, it can tolerate a great deal of sun.

Landscape Uses: This is a good fern to mass under deciduous trees or on moist hillsides. It is especially useful in sites that receive both a lot of sun and shade because it will tolerate both extremes. Its small size and evergreen nature make it a valuable plant for a rock garden as well.

Insects and Diseases: Christmas fern has no serious pests or diseases.

Polystichum acrostichoides

BULBS

Caladium x hortulanum

Caladium x hortulanum

COMMON NAME:
CALADIUM

Family: Araceae
Hardiness: To Zone 10
Shade Tolerance/Preference:
Light or partial shade

Habit and Mature Size: Caladiums grow 1 to 2 feet (30.5 to 61cm) tall, depending upon the cultivar, and about 2 feet (61cm) wide.

Aesthetic Value: Caladiums are tuberous plants that are grown for their bold, tropical foliage. The leaves are large, typically 8 to 12 inches (20.5 to 30.5cm) long, and either heart- or arrow-shaped. Colors range from silvery white to pale pink to deep red, and many forms are multicolored.

Cultural Needs: Caladiums are tropical by nature and like a warm climate and moist, reasonably fertile soil. They should be considered tender in most regions and set outside only when there is no danger of frost. When the leaves die down in the autumn, they should be allowed to ripen and the plant should be allowed to go dormant. The tubers can then be dug up and stored inside in a cool, dry place until the following spring.

Landscape Uses: Caladiums make a dramatic statement planted in a container or in a shady corner of the garden. They can be eye-catching either planted in groups or as a single specimen. The silvery and pale green forms are especially effective in brightening a dark area and easing the transition between different colors and kinds of plants.

Insects and Diseases: Caladiums have no serious pests or diseases.

Cultivars: 'Carolyn Wharton' has large pink leaves with deep rose veins and dark green splotches along the edges. 'June Bride' has silvery-white leaves with pale green veins and green margins. 'Rosalie' has multihued leaves in vibrant shades of deep red, pale pink, light green, and darker green along the edges.

Colchicum autumnale

COMMON NAME:
AUTUMN CROCUS

Family: Liliaceae
Hardiness: To Zone 5
Shade Tolerance/Preference:
Light or partial shade

Habit and Mature Size: Grows 4 to 8 inches (10 to 20.5cm) tall.

Aesthetic Value: The great appeal of this hardy bulb is the time of year in which it blooms. As the name suggests, autumn crocus blooms in autumn. Mauve or white flowers, single or double depending upon the cultivar, rise up on stout white stems totally devoid of leaves. The flowers are 2 to 8 inches (5 to 20.5cm) wide and flowering persists over a few weeks. Only months later, in early spring, does the foliage appear. The leaves are deep green, straplike in form and grow about 12 inches (30.5cm) tall. They die back several weeks after first emerging.

Cultural Needs: Crocuses are not demanding when it comes to soil conditions. The corms should be planted in late summer or very early fall when dormant. Plant them 3 to 4 inches (7.5 to 10cm) deep and 6 to 9 inches (15 to 23cm) apart. The corms are poisonous. Allow the foliage to yellow and die naturally in the spring.

Colchicum autumnale

121

Landscape Uses: Plant crocuses within groundcover plantings for best effect. If grown within a bed of periwinkle or sweet woodruff, for example, the dying spring foliage can be effectively hidden and the emerging flowers in autumn do not look quite so naked. In cool climates they will eventually naturalize.

Insects and Diseases: Autumn crocus has no serious pests or diseases.

Cultivars: 'Album' has single, clean white flowers. 'Pleniflorum' grows 4 to 6 inches (10 to 15cm) tall and has double, purplish pink flowers.

Crocus tomasinianus

COMMON NAME:
TOMMY CROCUS

Family: Iridaceae / **Hardiness:** To Zones 4 or 5
Shade Tolerance/Preference: Light shade or full sun

Habit and Mature Size: Tommy crocus grows 4 inches (10cm) high.

Crocus tomasinianus

Aesthetic Value: This crocus species has slender lilac to purple flowers with a white throat. It blooms in early spring.

Cultural Needs: This species of crocus is very hardy. It increases rapidly enough that the squirrels and other rodents who tend to devastate great drifts of many species of crocus never manage to ravage the Tommy crocus. It does prefer a soil that is consistently moist.

Landscape Uses: Plant this crocus in large groups within groundcovers or allow it to naturalize in a lawn for early spring interest. If planted in the latter, do not mow the grass until the crocus foliage has begun to die down.

Insects and Diseases: Squirrels and rodents may feed on crocuses.

Cultivars: 'Barr's Purple' has large, deep purple flowers, seeds freely, and is resistant to squirrels and other rodents. 'Roseus' blooms in February or March and has rosy lilac flowers.

Galanthus nivalis

COMMON NAME:
COMMON SNOWDROP

Family: Amaryllidaceae / **Hardiness:** Zones 3–9
Shade Tolerance/Preference: Light or partial shade or sun

Habit and Mature Size: Common snowdrops grow 6 inches (15cm) tall and spread 2 to 3 inches (5 to 7.5cm) wide.

Aesthetic Value: This diminutive bulb is one of the loveliest harbingers of spring. It is not unusual for snowdrops to bloom while snow is still on the ground. From each bulb two or three flat, narrow, deep green leaves emerge along with a slightly arching stem. The flowers dangle at the tips of the stems. Flowers are bright white and each of the shorter, inner petals has a green tip.

Cultural Needs: Snowdrops prefer a well-drained, average soil. They should be planted in autumn and will be most effective if planted in large groups.

Landscape Uses: Snowdrops are best used in large drifts of a hundred or more bulbs. Plant them where they can be seen and appreciated when they bloom in late winter.

Galanthus nivalis

They are glorious under deciduous trees, planted among an evergreen groundcover, or allowed to naturalize in a lawn. If grown in turf, do not mow until the snowdrop leaves have turned yellow.

Insects and Diseases: Snowdrops have no serious pests or diseases.

Cultivars: 'Florepleno' has double white flowers.

Hyacinthoides hispanica (a.k.a. Endymion hispanicus or Scilla campanulata)

COMMON NAME:
SPANISH BLUEBELLS

Family: Liliaceae / **Hardiness:** Zones 4–8
Shade Tolerance/Preference: Light or partial shade or sun

Habit and Mature Size: This bulb grows 15 to 20 inches (38 to 51cm) high and forms a sprawling clump.

Aesthetic Value: Spanish bluebells have numerous wide, bell-shaped blue flowers that are held on slender stems. There are forms available with white, pink, or lilac-blue flowers as well. The leaves are long, leathery, and straplike.

Cultural Needs: Spanish bluebells like a well-drained soil with organic matter added. They are not at all fussy or demanding. The bulbs should be planted in autumn, 3 to 4 inches (7.5 to 10cm) deep and 4 to 6 inches (10 15cm) apart. They go dormant by midsummer and the foliage should be retained until then.

Landscape Uses: Spanish bluebells are wonderful bulbs to naturalize along the edge of a woodland in deciduous shade. They are tough and colorful and make a lovely sight when grown in large sweeps.

Insects and Diseases: White-tailed deer will eat the flowers and leaves.

Cultivars: 'Blue Queen' has pale blue flowers in May. 'Rose Queen' has clear pink flowers. 'White Triumphator' is a strong grower with bright white flowers.

Lycoris squamigera

COMMON NAMES:
MAGIC LILY, HARDY AMARYLLIS

Family: Amaryllidaceae
Hardiness: Zones 5–9
Shade Tolerance/Preference: Light or partial shade

Habit and Mature Size: Leafless stems grow 2 to 3 feet (61cm to 1m) tall.

Aesthetic Value: In late summer to early autumn this little-known bulb sends up erect stems topped with large, airy clusters of long-petaled rosy pink flowers. The flowers are fragrant and look like very delicate lilies. The foliage at the base of the plant is broad and daffodillike. The leaves emerge several weeks after the flowers fade. They elongate in spring and die back to the ground in summer, approximately one to two months before the new flowers appear.

Cultural Needs: Magic lily likes well-drained, average soil. Bulbs should be planted in midsummer, before the

Lycoris squamigera

flower stems appear. Place the bulbs 5 to 6 inches (12.5 to 15cm) deep and 6 inches (15cm) apart and keep the plants well watered during dry spells in autumn and spring.

Landscape Uses: The flowers of magic lily always seem like a wonderful surprise when they suddenly appear just as many plants are beginning to languish. This is an excellent plant to use along a woodland path or within a ground cover planting under deciduous trees. It is delicate and graceful and the blooms are splendid as cut flowers.

Insects and Diseases: Magic lily has no serious pests or diseases.

Scilla sibirica

COMMON NAME:

SIBERIAN SQUILL

Family: Liliaceae / **Hardiness:** Zones 3–8

Shade Tolerance/Preference:

Light or partial shade or full sun

Habit and Mature Size: Siberian squill grows 6 inches (15cm) tall and 2 to 3 inches (5 to 7.5cm) wide.

Aesthetic Value: This hardy bulb blooms early in the spring. Deep blue, star-shaped flowers appear in clusters on tiny, leafless stems. The leaves are bright green and straplike and persist unobtrusively until early summer.

Cultural Needs: Plant Siberian squills in autumn approximately 3 to 4 inches (7.5 to 10cm) deep. They will be most effective if planted in large quantities in average, well-drained soil. This plant never needs to be divided and is in every respect carefree.

Landscape Uses: Siberian squills are delightful placed in drifts under trees and shrubs, especially if planted along with other spring-flowering plants. A large grouping under a white-flowered magnolia, for example, is breathtaking as the fallen blossoms of the magnolia mix with the sky blue flowers of the squills.

Insects and Diseases: Siberian squill has no serious pests or diseases.

Cultivars: 'Alba' blooms early and has pure white flowers. 'Spring Beauty' has exquisite blue flowers.

Scilla sibirica

Plant Hardiness Zone Map

RANGE OF AVERAGE
ANNUAL MINIMUM
TEMPERATURES FOR
EACH ZONE

ZONE 1 BELOW –50° F
ZONE 2 –50° TO –40°
ZONE 3 –40° TO –30°
ZONE 4 –30° TO –20°
ZONE 5 –20° TO –10°
ZONE 6 –10° TO   0°
ZONE 7   0° TO 10°
ZONE 8   10° TO 20°
ZONE 9   20° TO 30°
ZONE 10 30° TO 40°
ZONE 11 ABOVE 40°

125

Sources

While few if any nurseries specialize in shade plants, you can find shade-loving species at any nursery or garden center, and in the catalogs of almost every mail-order supplier.

UNITED STATES

Busse Gardens
Route 2, Box 238
Cokato, MN 55321
Extensive listing of popular perennials

Gardens of the Blue Ridge
9056 Pittman Gap Road
P.O. Box 10
Pineola, NC 28662
Excellent selection of native trees and shrubs

Jackson & Perkins
P.O. Box 1028
Medford, OR 97501
Fine selection of plants for shade

Kurt Bluemel, Inc.
2740 Green Lane
Baldwin, MD 31013
Excellent selection of ornamental grasses, rushes, and sedges

Morden Nurseries, Ltd.
P.O. Box 1270
Morden, MB
Canada R0G 1J0
Wide selection of ornamental trees and shrubs

Shepherd's Garden Seeds
30 Irene Street
Torrington, CT 06790
Fine selection of annuals and perennials

Wayside Gardens
Garden Lande
Hodges, SC 29695
Offers a wide array of bulbs and perennials

Westgate Garden Nursery
751 Westgate Drive
Eureka, CA 95503
Large selection of rhododendrons and unusual ornamental shrubs and trees

White Flower Farm
P.O. Box 50
Litchfield, CT 06759
Good selection of shade plants, including hostas, ferns, and hellebores

Van Engelen Inc.
23 Tulip Drive
Bantam, CT 06750
Wide variety of bulbs

AUSTRALIA

Country Farm Perennials
RSD Laings Road
Nayook VIC 3821

Cox's Nursery
RMB 216 Oaks Road
Thrilmere NSW 2572

Honeysuckle Cottage Nursery
Lot 35 Bowen Mountain Road
Bowen Mountain via Grosevale NSW 2753

CANADA

Corn Hill Nursery Ltd.
RR 5
Petitcodiac NB EOA 2HO

Ferncliff Gardens
SS 1
Mission, British Columbia
V2V 5V6

McFayden Seed Co. Ltd.
Box 1800
Brandon, Manitoba
R7A 6N4

Stirling Perennials
RR 1
Morpeth, Ontario
N0P 1X0

Photo Credits

©**Harriet L. Cramer**: pp. 23, 31 right

©**Crandall & Crandall**: p. 26

©**R. Todd Davis**: pp. 18, 68, 92, 99, 104, 106-107, 124 left

Dembinsky Photo Associates: ©John Gerlach: p. 118 right

©**Ken Druse/The Natural Garden**: pp. 27 bottom, 60, 83, 108, 115

Envision: ©Bart Barlow: p. 35 left; ©George Livadaras: pp. 75 right, 101 left; ©Steve Pace: p. 111

©**John Glover**: pp. 1, 2, 8, 11, 13 both, 15, 22, 30, 33, 45, 56, 58, 59, 66 left, 73 right, 89, 101 right, 113, 121

©**judywhite/New Leaf Images**: pp. 24 bottom left, 66 right, 70

©**Dency Kane**: pp. 12 top, 16, 24 top left, 27 top, 31 left, 47 top, 51, 52 left, 73 left, 77, 80 right, 85, 100, 102, 103 both, 105 right, 116, 120, 123

©**image/dennis krukowski**: Designer: Carol Guthrie: p. 6

©**Robert E. Lyons**: pp. 41, 64, 107 right

©**Allan Mandell**: pp. 17, 40

©**Charles Mann**: pp. 10, 12 bottom left & right, 20, 24 top right, 28 both, 29, 76, 78 left, 84 left, 86, 87, 88 right, 93 right

Maslowski Wildlife Productions: p. 9

©**Clive Nichols**: Greencombe Garden, Somerset: p. 14; pp. 24 bottom right, 50, 57, 65, 69, 71, 88 left, 93 left, 94, 97, 98 both, 122, 124 right

©**Jerry Pavia**: pp. 34 bottom, 35 right, 37, 43, 44, 52 right, 55 both, 61, 62, 63, 74-75, 78 right, 81, 91 right, 109, 110, 112, 119

©**Joanne Pavia**: pp. 38, 95, 105 left, 114

Photo/Nats, Inc.: ©Liz Ball: p. 117; ©Cathy Wilkinson Barash: p. 42; ©Gay Bumgarner: p. 36; ©Priscilla Connell: pp. 21, 32; ©Gregory Crisci: p. 118 left; ©Wally Eberhart: p. 82; ©Betsy Fuchs: p. 84 right; ©Hal Horwitz: pp. 39, 67 left, 91 left, 96-97; ©John A. Lynch: p. 80 left; ©Robert E. Lyons: pp. 49, 79; ©Ben Phillips: pp. 48, 67 right; ©Ann Reilly: pp. 19, 47 bottom; ©David M. Stone: pp. 53, 54; ©Virginia Twinam-Smith: pp. 34 top, 38 top

Index